The Result Is What You See Today

The Result Is What You See Today

Poems about Running

smith|doorstop

Published 2019 by
Smith|Doorstop books
The Poetry Business
Campo House
54 Campo Lane
Sheffield S1 2EG
www.poetrybusiness.co.uk

ISBN 978-1-912196-81-4

British Library Cataloguing-in-Publication Data.
A catalogue record for this book is available from the
British Library.

Designed and Typeset by Utter
Cover image by Tim Morris
Printed and bound by CPI Group (UK) Ltd, Croydon, CR0 4YY

Smith|Doorstop is a member of Inpress,
www.inpressbooks.co.uk. Distributed by NBN International, Airport Business
Centre, 10 Thornbury Road Plymouth PL 6 7PP.

The Poetry Business receives financial support from
Arts Council England

Supported by
ARTS COUNCIL
ENGLAND

Contents

11 Introductions

CHARLES HAMILTON SORLEY
19 The Song of the Ungirt Runners

'what I was born for'

MICHAEL BROWN
23 Lap

ALISON BINNEY
23 Night Run

JOE CALDWELL
24 People Who Go Running

TRACEY HERD
25 What I Remember

VICKI HUSBAND
25 Something more considerable

JON MCLEOD
26 Running – a bucket list

NICKY HALLETT
27 The Experienced Huntsman.
With instructions for Hunting the
Buck, the Hare, the Fox, the Badger,
the Marten, and the Otter (1780)

NELL FARRELL
28 Running on Silloth Beach on
Christmas Day

CYNTHIA X HUA
28 Mile Time

ALAN PAYNE
30 A Local Legend

WENDY PRATT
30 Fuck You

KATE NOAKES
32 A run up to the course of love

JENNY KING
33 Runners in Town

MORAG SMITH
33 The Tuesday night joggers

JATINDER PADDA
34 On Running

MIKE DI PLACIDO
35 Losing It

VICTORIA GATEHOUSE
35 Eight Hundred Metres

CAROLE BROMLEY
37 Sprint

VERITY OCKENDEN
38 Battle Cry

STEPHEN LIGHTBOWN
38 Hitting the Berlin Wall

ELISABETH SENNITT CLOUGH
40 Parkrun

RIVER WOLTON
41 Run

LYNNE REES
42 I am running through the
wondrous silence of history

JOHN GOODBY
42 The Tough of the Track: an Alf
Tupper triptych

MARK FIDDES
45 Lane Discipline

MARK GRANIER
46 Stopwatch

BARRY TENCH
46 Cross Country

DUNCAN CHAMBERS
47 Thornes Park, Wakefield

PETER SANSOM
48 Cross Country

'against the rising light'

PINDAR, TRANSLATED BY FRANK NISETICH
53 *from* Olympian XI (*Pindar's Victory Songs*)

JAN HERITAGE
53 Yes Tor Hill Race

ERIC CHANDLER
54 20180611 Sacramento 4 miles

HELEN MORT
55 Fox Miles

LAURA MCKEE
55 Alnitak, Alnilam and Mintaka

LIZ LEFROY
56 Running Advice

OLIVER COMINS
57 Jogging

JANE ASPINALL
58 10k

STUART PICKFORD
58 Hill

NIALL CAMPBELL
59 A New Father Thinks About Those Running Home

ALAN BUCKLEY
60 Run

NATALIE WHITTAKER
61 The ring-necked parakeets of South East London

PAUL STEPHENSON
62 The Result is What You See Today

IGOR KLIKOVAC, TRANSLATED BY JOHN MCAULIFFE
63 Gratitude to Big Cities

MARK CONNORS
64 On the tops

HELEN MORT
65 Coffin Path

GEOFF COX
66 Early Start, Winter Run. impression sequence

ALWYN MARRIAGE
67 Morning Run

RACHAEL MEAD
67 The dog, the blackbird and the anxious mind

SUZANNE CONWAY
68 Coach

RAE HOWELLS
69 School Run

DIANE MULHOLLAND
70 The Ultra Runner

BETH MCDONOUGH
70 Tempting the Runner Off the Green Circular, Dundee

NELL FARRELL
71 Blessing at the Allotments

LIZZY TURNER
72 trajectory

DIANA MOEN PRITCHARD
72 Forest Run

JONATHAN MAYMAN
73 phantom runner

STUART PICKFORD
74 Running Against Wordsworth

LIZZIE HOLDEN
75 Spring Run

SARAH PASSINGHAM
75 In my treads

WENDY PRATT
76 Godsong

GILES GOODLAND
76 The Canal Path

IFOR THOMAS
77 Autumn Run

PAM THOMPSON
78 Running, Anglesey, Easter

MATTHEW WEST
79 Evening Out

JULIE MELLOR
80 Ghosts

OLGA DERMOTT-BOND
80 In Sickness and In Health

'our bodies gone to our heads'

A E HOUSMAN
85 To an Athlete Dying Young

RACHEL BOWER
86 Run for your life

MARA ADAMITZ SCRUPE
86 On Winning the Marathon
at Sixty

BEN NORRIS
88 Big Heart

ROBERT WALTON
89 Re-Run

ALAN PAYNE
90 Sprinter

NOEL CONNOR
91 The Gap

PAT EDWARDS
92 Spider

ANTHONY COSTELLO
92 Running Pacts

STUART HANDYSIDES
93 The rite of autumn

JACK HOUSTON
94 Sunny September Days

MIKE FARREN
95 Running with Simon, 1983

JULIA FORSTER
95 Running with Mums

SUZANNE CONWAY
96 Winter Training

MARK GRANIER
97 Night Run, Mount Merrion, 1975

JULIE LUMSDEN
98 DASH

JON MCLEOD
98 The Middle Miles

JOSIE ALFORD
99 An Exercise in How to Move On

M R PEACOCKE
100 Running

MARK CARSON
100 Not running but failing

LORRAINE MARINER
101 Tritina for My Hips

JULIAN BISHOP
101 Treadmill

LEWIS BUXTON
102 Fragility

ABEER AMEER
103 The Runner

DAVID BORROTT
104 Hainault Road

PAUL HOWARTH
104 it's when the body is at its most

like a machine that the mind is at its

least like a machine

RACHAEL MEAD
106 Outdoor drum solo

NICHOLAS MCGAUGHEY
106 Trainers

TERRY QUINN
107 to my red tracksuit top

ROB WALTON
108 Spanner Skills

PAUL STEPHENSON
109 Urban Wildlife

ANNA WOODFORD
110 Bedsocks; Willow

'I won't stop until I've travelled from one life to another'

GEOFFREY HILL
113 *from* Watching the Boston Marathon

MARIA TAYLOR
113 Woman Running Alone

MARIE PAPIER
114 Run, Boorana, Run ...

SCOTT PALMIERI
115 The Ex-Convict Runs a 10k

PAM THOMPSON
116 The Run

JUSTINA HART
117 Running

KATIE GREENBROWN
118 Someone else's bum

KERRY DARBISHIRE
120 Flight

CAROLE BROMLEY
121 Twelve Reasons Why Not

IAIN TWIDDY
121 Thawing River

OLGA DERMOTT-BOND
122 M25, turning

STEPHEN LIGHTBOWN
122 Running Together in Greenwich Park

STUART BARNES
124 Running In The Family

VICTORIA GATEHOUSE
125 Snails

‘

MANDY SUTTER
125 Old Trail Runner

DI SLANEY
126 Bildr's thorp

KATHARINE GODA
127 Running Away

ESTELLE PRICE
128 Running after dark in Homa Bay
County

JON MCLEOD
128 Blake on his morning run sees
angels in a tree

RISHI DASTIDAR
129 Unhalting

GILES GOODLAND
130 Sewage

JULIE MACLEAN
131 Thread Lines

LORRAINE MARINER
132 Running, Like an Old Flame

HELEN ALLISON
133 Culbin Forest 5K

SARAH VENART
133 I Believe You Still Have My Key

LUCY HOLT
134 once you're on you can't get off

LYDIA ALLISON
135 Inevitable

ANNE RYLAND
136 Sunday, on the run

ERIN WILSON
137 Running as Birdsong

139 About the authors

159 Acknowledgements

162 Index of poem and first lines

Diane Leather

The first woman to run a sub-five-minute mile.

1933 – 2018

Introductions

Kim Moore

I've been working as a freelance poet for the last couple of years which involves a lot of travel and overnight stays in hotels. Although I love my job, perhaps some of my most enduring memories from the last few years come from the times in between running a workshop or giving a reading. Invariably I go out for a run as a way of finding myself in a strange city. I go alone if I have to, but I prefer to find another poet-runner to go with. As you can see from this anthology, there's a thriving community of poet-runners around, if you know where to look.

Throughout the editing and selection process I've been thinking about the similarities between running and writing – how I use both to find out what I think about something, or what I know-without-knowing. They both have a contradiction at their heart, rooted in the individual act, yet for me at least, they have to take place within a living thriving community.

It's been a real honour to read the hundreds of poems that were submitted. Each one felt like a window into another life, another run, another race. They are poems about running, but they're about so much more. They are about freedom and the body, about pain and our relationship to the world around us, about childhood memories, friendships and ageing, politics and gender and society, self-image, dreaming and limits.

Many of the poems contained within these pages circle round the central question of why we run at all, and the conclusion must be that there are as many reasons as there are runners. My own relationship with running changed whilst working on this anthology as I became more and more pregnant. My runs got slower and shorter. I stopped worrying about getting faster, and instead started to enjoy running as a privilege which enabled me to ground myself in the world around me, and feel more connected to my changing body and the strange passenger I carried inside.

This idea of running being a transformative act is explored in the fourth section of the anthology: 'I won't stop until I've travelled from one life to another'. There are poems that explore the idea of the self being transformed by running, as well as the many ways our relationship with running can be transformed. The third section of the anthology 'Our bodies gone to our heads' examines the role of the body – how it carries us through pain and difficulty, and how it can let us down. The second section of the anthology is titled 'Against the rising light' and examines perhaps one of the central reasons why many people run – as a way of being present in the world and connecting with the environment. Finally, the first section 'What I was born for' is made up of those poems which seemed to us to try and articulate the reasons for running. Many of them concern themselves with being 'in the moment'. Of course, many of the poems could have sat in different sections – we hope these possibilities and connections will keep readers moving through the anthology.

Finally, we hope you enjoy reading the poems as much as we enjoyed reading, discussing and selecting them and that they inspire you to run, or to write a poem or both.

Paul Deaton

I live in the dynamic, frenetic, creative city Bristol: a place currently going through a running renaissance judging by the swell in numbers at my club and the running events in and around this city. Bristol is an ethnically diverse, generally alternative, sea-faring, self-made place; that's been down, as many cities have, but now given an influx of recent nationalities particularly from the Latin countries Spain and Italy, it's on the up. It is a place a stone's throw from London that attracts people who like cities but who wish to live an outdoor-type-life: climbers, cyclists, triathletes (Chrissie Wellington lives just outside) and runners, who abound along the broken pavements, the worn parkland limestone trails, the industrial hinterlands, the canal, the cycle-paths, the wide expanse of the Downs, the various city's Victorian steps, the floating harbour, and the Avon's snaking towpath and port-way out to the Severn.

I happen to run with one of the Bristol clubs, Southville RC. (It hasn't always been this way. This club. Or me running with one). I've heard it often said by people at my club, when I've been chatting one on one, in a quiet reflective moment, that the runner declaims 'they don't do clubs,' that they are not, in-spite of running out with the club, a clubby-type-of-person. In fact, I'd stretch this admission, which might well be my projection, that most are and feel themselves to be, as far as clubs go, to a degree outsiders – or more positively, one might say, people who have found in running something similar that holds them fast to the varied life experiences they've encountered. Now the second thing I've noticed, which no doubt won't apply to everyone, but does apply to many people here, is that running is in someway a personal 'cure' to experiences so powerful that they've had to, in some way, refigure their lives: illness, bereavement, break-ups; all sorts of hard, put-upon, life changing hurts and ups and downs that have resulted in reassessment, that have resulted in running. Here they've found a stress-busting outlet, a structure that allows them expression to live well and live again, and with each run – again and again – to move forwards in life that strengthens and does not reduce them. So yes, my club is a club, but you'll find in general it is a club run by and used by people, individuals, who say they don't do clubs, perhaps the word community would be far better. The community thrives on this difference of the individual – a collective dis-cohesion – and this is similar, perhaps even the same, as this anthology of running poems.

Here you'll find a collection of poems that we have savoured, but it is a collection of poems by poets who have faced something in themselves, beyond the running and beyond using words and being poets; the poetry and the running are merely the means, the transmutation of getting back into, and re-entering a fluid-flow with life. It is, to quote northerner Tony Harrison, a 'ceremony of articulation,' and in this ceremony, all of life appears to surface.

So here read in full that saturated with life fluid-flow: regrets, triumphs, losses, epiphanies, memories, streams of consciousness, absorption into nature, into one's body, a wholeness, and rich beautiful fleetingness into the universe, that pulses both in and out of focus, appears at times in HD as the blood has pumped through veins, in the zinging, endorphin-enriched brain, and the self that appears suddenly, like sunshine after rain in technicolour, in unspeakable brilliance, this might be as simple as sunlight falling on a decaying wall, or the way the leaves in the sycamore tree are waving like small shaking hands. Here are poems with just these small details. Once you have felt this fullness, the running buzz, then here becomes the positive addiction. You want it again and again. The perfect easy run. The poem that says it all or says all it can about one moment. These are poems not on the way to becoming but that have achieved their goal. A collection of varied, disparate and individual voices. But all sharing the same root cause and a liberation in an activity that at its best transcends circumstance and brings the person back into the heartfelt truth of themselves and the nearby, closely-experienced earth.

Poetry and running. Perfect bedfellows. A perfect test of who we are. Byron knew of such a test when, in 1810, he swam the Hellespont, and regarded it his best achievement; the test offered an enlargement of who he was. Byron style – and who he thought he was! It was this test, crossing from Europe to Asia, though, and not his poems, he most alluded to. The poets assembled here would know about this. And Byron, knowing what he found in swimming, perhaps, well, he could've been induced to run regularly the local parkrun or more probably an ultra-marathon – but sadly, he had a club foot.

Enjoy the poems. We did.

Ben Wilkinson

Running is pointless. Where our Stone Age ancestors ran great distances across the plains in pursuit of food – scavenging and so-called 'persistence hunting', i.e. tiring out less hardy prey – we now live in a mechanised world that allows us to travel and transport at speeds and over distances incomprehensible to early man. In fact, when it comes to speed, as a species we're not even particularly good at it: the average warthog could beat Usain Bolt at his 100m-world-record-setting best. Even elite athletes generate more energy as heat than as forward motion. Looked at like this, running can seem tiring, frustrating and unnecessary. Anyone who runs will have faced the question at least once: *Why do you bother?*

Bill Bowerman, University of Oregon running coach, was fond of philosophising to his fresh-faced varsity recruits. 'Running, one might say, is basically an absurd pastime on which to be exhausting ourselves', he would suggest. 'But if you can find meaning in the type of running you need to do, chances are you'll be able to find meaning in that other absurd pastime: life'. So the question of why we variously run is really the bigger question of why we do anything at all, in a world that – unless you're deeply religious in some way – can look to be without much meaning.

I'm writing this at a time when running, in all its forms, is in rude health. Two million adults in England alone go running at least once a week. The parkrun initiative – free, weekly, timed 5k events open to all, and likely in a park near you – started as a small get-together in 2004; 15 years later there are over five million registered parkrunners worldwide. As my co-editors Paul and Kim also suggest, there might be as many reasons for running as runners themselves: for fitness; for self-esteem and recovery; for competition (with yourself and/or others); as a brief, clarifying escape from the pressures and demands of modern life. But I'd also like to propose that most runners who return to running throughout their lives tend to do so because it helps them, as Bowerman suggests, to 'find meaning' – to make sense of themselves and the world around them. And in that respect, running has a lot in common with poetry.

Haruki Murakami once claimed that most of what he knows about writing he learned by running every day. There's a long history of running writers: Jonathan Swift, Joyce Carol Oates, Andre Dubus, Don DeLillo, to name a few. For me, running and writing poetry have become two sides of the same finisher's medal. Despite the sometime company and camaraderie, both are fundamentally solitary pursuits. With running it's you versus the path ahead, you versus your ambitions. In poetry it's you versus the blank page, you versus the many ways in which words and language might fail. But it's also, in both disciplines, you pitted against yourself, your angels and demons, your hopes and fears and dreams. Writing a poem, you're trying to reach beyond the borders of speech, the limits of words and their meaning, and the best poets somehow manage it, putting into words what can't be put into words – until it is. Running, you're trying to stretch beyond the limits of the self, your apparent capabilities, and watching the best athletes, at amateur and professional level alike, they seem to outrun the constraints of the human mind and body – they almost transcend the physical as a great poem almost transcends the language. The margins for success can be slim, the chances of failure high. With that in mind, the unlikely communities that running fosters are much like those among poets, and probably spring up for the same reasons. Solidarity, mutual recognition of determination and effort, achievement in the face of the odds. No wonder we need clubs.

But all of that is to talk in terms of running and writing as a kind of purposeful achievement: in pursuit of 'success', however personal and relative it might be. The poems in this anthology are successes, but they are also a wonderful and much broader testament to the ways in which running and the creative act of placing words on a page coincide: routine, connection, insight, transformation, joy, even defiance. And play. Running, like writing a poem, might sometimes be done for the sake of something else; in that respect, it would be typical of what the philosopher and runner Mark Rowlands calls 'our narrowly instrumental age'. But if the poems we've gathered in these pages collectively test a single idea, it's that poetry and running – rhythmical, escapist; in part, always rebellious – are best and truest when done purely for their own sake. In the first and final instance, runners run as writers write: because they want to, and because they can.

CHARLES HAMILTON SORLEY

The Song of the Ungirt Runners

We swing ungirded hips,
And lightened are our eyes,
The rain is on our lips,
We do not run for prize.
We know not whom we trust
Nor whitherward we fare,
But we run because we must
    Through the great wide air.

The waters of the seas
Are troubled as by storm.
The tempest strips the trees
And does not leave them warm.
Does the tearing tempest pause?
Do the tree-tops ask it why?
So we run without a cause
    'Neath the big bare sky.

The rain is on our lips,
We do not run for prize.
But the storm the water whips
And the wave howls to the skies.
The winds arise and strike it
And scatter it like sand,
And we run because we like it
    Through the broad bright land.

'what I was born for'

MICHAEL BROWN
Lap

Suppose in the rain when you run
you think of breath,
the kilometre kiss-kiss of rubber
on asphalt,
your own cage of pain –

what if no thought
of else or other
comes to enter
the repeated metres repeated metres
lapped in limbic dark?

ALISON BINNEY
Night Run

The thought of it has trailed me all day
like a cooped-up dog, and now my tea's
gone down, I've washed up, watched
the news, I could check my emails again
but know if I give the sofa an inch
it will take a mile – three, actually,
those three I've promised myself
since I didn't go yesterday or the day before,
so it's on with the fluorescent top
and I'm pulling my calf socks up,
thinking I've done the hard bit now,
anything else is a bonus, coaxing my toes
into trainers and out of the front door.
The air's cold enough to gnaw on,
the street so quiet I'm running in velvet
slippers, and it's already worth it,
taking the blind corner a little too fast,

playing roulette with the cyclist
who's never there, endorphins pumping
my arms into superhero fists, feet skipping
the cracks I can't even see. I'm all breath
and blood. Frost prickles my thumbs.
I dart between amber pools, slick as a fish,
know as I leap from the kerb there won't be a car,
not when I'm this invincible, yes, for this
is what I was born for, this bright air,
the whole tingle and spring of it all,
flinging me into the night.

JOE CALDWELL

People Who Go Running

can be recognised in various ways;
but don't worry, they'll tell you. They're forever
synchronising their complicated watches,
or shopping for expensive trainers that
a physio said would be good for their arches.

They dream of fast courses and negative splits,
though not for too long as they've set the alarm
to go trail running as the ripe sun
spreads itself out across the Peak District.

If you live with them, they'll forget to make dinner
as they're busy signing up for half marathons
in Clowne and Stamford. They'll bookmark Strava
on your laptop and commandeer a drawer
for vests and gels and spiky massage balls.

They'll come home from long runs in winter
and breathe joy into the cold air, morning
fizzing through their veins and sweat settling
on their skin like a beginning, like glory.

TRACEY HERD

What I Remember

is not the race itself but the evening
which disappeared in a tangle of diving
sunlight and nerves as I hugged myself,
chilled, and waited for the starter, bent
forward, the tang of mown grass
sprayed like water and the white lines
freshly painted on the spongy red track,
breasting the tape, alone and splendid,
queen of my own universe, then the medal
like a tiny sun catching the last of the light,
and feeling as if my heart would burst.

VICKI HUSBAND

Something more considerable

*... For my friends who run long distances, these tiny fragments of levitation
add up to something more considerable; by their own power they hover above
the earth for many minutes, perhaps some significant portion of an hour ...*
– Rebecca Solnit

Begin by leaving yourself behind; forget what you know
and start to run. Be quick to tune out the slap of your feet
on tarmac, and the respiratory soundtrack, that remind you
of the force you fight to maintain an act of h o v e r i n g.

Focus on the small but significant space between you and
planet earth. Briefest aeronaut you have a unique perspective
you could almost make a life within this near-earth orbit, station
a second home in its high hinterlands, grow aeroponically, foster
as many clouds as you dare: watch them leave home by the hour,
hear from them years later happily trapped in arctic ice.

But levitation – as a destination in its own right – should be free
from encumbrance, your mind untaxed, unornamented.
Contemplate instead the quanta of air that you tread on:
not each solitary one so much as their more considerable sum.

JON MCLEOD

Running – a bucket list

Early Cretaceous, gentle jog amongst tree ferns and a herd of grazing
Iguanodon.

Cave system at Lascaux, circa 15,000 BC, quicker pace this time but slow
enough to be depicted as a stick figure in ash and ochre.

Hill run with Moses, stone tablets providing full body workout.

The battle of Prestonpans, 21 September 1745, joining the Highland
Charge, downhill sprint session, avoiding musket fire.

The foredeck of a supertanker, mid-Pacific, pace intervals in the sea fret,
bottle of whisky.

The ninth circle of hell, club run led by Dante and fellow sinners, difficult
footing on icy lake.

Jupiter, a tricky half-marathon, taking it easy in the swirling gas vortex.

The mind of the Zen monk, Wumen Huikai, steady run through the
Gateless Gate, home for tea.

NICKY HALLETT

The Experienced Huntsman. With instructions for Hunting the Buck, the Hare, the Fox, the Badger, the Marten, and the Otter (1780)

he who undertakes to be a huntsman to a lord or gentleman
ought to be an active sharp expert fellow
to be a good horseman
and be fleet of foot

by reason that very often he is obliged to go two or three miles
running
to find game through mountains bogs mosses and rank coverts
where a horse cannot ride

and this the obligation to a man
with one leg or with two
as well as those supplemented pinionly by their mounts' limbs
whether riding or on Shanks' pony

that even the wood-legged cross-countrier
might pursue as best he can
out-pace all manner of creatures
and not only those animals listed but others as yet unknown by name

that he may assume the qualities of those brutes
to entirely empathise
to blood-boundedly brother them
and by cunning utterly understand what makes them tick

that he may on foot outwit them
as he does on horse
that he may race them
to their deaths

if not his own

NELL FARRELL

Running on Silloth Beach on Christmas Day

Counting hawks like magpies; three for a girl
curves like a comma, tucked in from the wind
on a bare branch by the road to Skinburness

and all the other place names catch your throat
like peat smoke: Calvo, Kelsick, Langrigg, Causewayhead.
The beach is wide and empty, snow glitters

on the hills across the Solway Firth.
I work my injured ankle like a racehorse
and the sand gives just enough. Sweating

I unravel arms from sleeves, billow, balance,
crush nothing, even though the ground is pocked
with purple mussel shells and icing sugar cockles.

I catch myself scanning for a stone,
the perfect souvenir, then think *Just run.*
The only thing you need from this is this itself.

CYNTHIA X HUA

Mile Time

I keep running through canyons, past houses,
the brain busy, hoping for the meaning
to appear in front of me like a flashcard.
I'm not sure why I left my job,
but I say over drinks at Black Flamingo
that something solid turned into a gas,
color flapped down onto the table,
and I wanted to be happier. I jog

unsteady, unsure across the overpass and wild turkeys
drift across the page like sheet music.
In the yellow pages,
it says to call and call soon, that
there's a reason for the order
we gave twenty-six letters. Today,
it looks like all the roadside flowers
are vanishing,
but it's hard to tell when things began to end.
A man I loved back then told me
that we're just dust particles
here to remember the beginning,
diagrams in the
textbook of physics.
When my mother calls,
I tell her I've taken up jogging,
that I'm making progress.
And I feel this body changing,
the leaves reddening.
On the phone, we agree to keep working at it,
that the equipment's complicated,
and we connect
somewhere on the inside
where it's harder to see the wires.
Meanwhile, the temperature drops
and the marathon runners
don their winter tracksuits,
neon pinks and greens,
swerving past me on the west loop,
holding down the ever-changing pace, the minute, the second,
like a hot air balloon. Vapor forms from breath,
and look how I've held on
to the time, the time, though I can't see it,
the numbers, the propane,
the looming end to another year, sharp tacks
rising with the air in my chest.

ALAN PAYNE

A Local Legend

I know a man who runs every day,
a tarmac addict, a city eccentric,
on the back of his faded tracksuit
a legend: URBAN AND SOBER.

He's been passing *The Fox and Hounds*
and *The Crown* for twenty-five years,
ever since he left a bottle
on the pavement outside *The Red Lion*.

He draws pictures of scenes he's seen on the streets,
gives them away to rough sleepers,
children playing truant, refugees,
anyone, like him, running for their lives.

WENDY PRATT

Fuck You

Yes, I'm fat, with a crooked nose
from an accident with a lamppost
and a slightly lazy eye and I look
(or so I'm told) the spitting dab
of my grandmother. I'm thirty-
seven and a bit. I am scarred, I am
scared, I am falling down drunk
on a Saturday night and too hungover
to leave the house. But I run. You
see me running, or jogging, or
dragging my fat arse along, puce
in my moon face, eyes watering,
fists clenched, sweating under

each swinging tit, gob gaping
because I'm fat and I am running.
Once upon a time I wore skirts
and bare legs and danced
in clubs and once upon a time
I wore skintight jeans and looked
so hot I set the house on fire. At twenty-
five I could have passed for sixteen
and when that cute little drug habit
kicked in I was the skinniest I've ever been.
And I remember that, like a drunken
dream. Not the stomach in knots
and the fingers down my throat
and the desperation to be thinner,
but the loose hips, lightheaded
high-as-a-kite girl with legs so long
they hurt your eyes and auburn hair
like Anne Boleyn. So, yeah, I've done
my time getting through and fighting on.
Now I am grown up and have a house,
and have a man, and when the things I loved,
I mean, the things I *really* loved, were gone,
despite me being so fucking good, all those
rearview mirror dreams, I fought. I fight on.
This? This training, this getting fitter,
this bringing myself back to something
I half recognise? This is nothing. Not to me.
So go on, laugh it up, turn away, whatever.
I don't give a fuck.

KATE NOAKES

A run up to the course of love

I can't run up the stairs,
but I can run a fever.

I can't run for a bus,
but I can run my mouth.

I can't run from sofa to 5k,
but I can run a risk.

I can't run the park,
but I can run late.

I can't run a half marathon,
but I can run with the hare and the hounds.

I can't run a whole marathon,
but I can run on empty.

I can't run the Pennine hills,
but I can run a company.

In the long run, rabbit,
you can run but you can't hide.

You are a running gag,
not born to run.

You've run to seed;
time for me to cut and run.

You were a hit and run;
I was running scared.

You're out of the running;
you can take a running jump.

JENNY KING
Runners in Town

Runners slip through the crowd, nip
round shopping-heavy pushchairs, on
past gossiping groups and are gone
into a sort of fourth dimension.

Hardly present, they slide
between minute and minute, intent
on escaping what time once meant,
while shoppers stare, asking each other

Was that Paul? Was that Sue? unsure
whether the flickering figures half seen
from behind might have been
the friends they knew, or thought they knew.

MORAG SMITH
The Tuesday night joggers

Every week, half past six we gather;
there's chatting, stretching, tightening of laces
till Dorothy arrives in purple lycra
and we lumber off, Kayleigh in the lead,
school champion at fifteen, pregnant at sixteen,
at thirty, twenty pounds and three kids wiser.
Close behind her, arms pumping, it's Yasmin,
washed up six months ago on a beach,
holding her life in a carrier bag;
there's Brenda giving up the ciggies again,
Pam just off the chemo and Kim with no English,
but we have our own language; the nod,
the smile, the high five, the total acceptance

of pink sequinned leggings. Shrugging off
car horns and jeering kids we pass the shops,
the big houses with their three-car driveways
the polished windows of other people's dreams.
Our dream is just to be here;
steady as the beat of a new heart,
soles slap the pavement, fat wobbles,
bladders cry out *we are full*,
but we've learned the art of just keeping going
and when we're out there I don't hear anybody
telling me I'm useless'll never do nothing;
when we're out here it's one perfect hour
of perspiration and gratification;
the world fades away
and it's just us, sweaty but invincible,
and faster than we used to be,
the Tuesday night sloggers, breaking free

JATINDER PADDA

On Running

Once I ran and the bracing damp air
Was the sweetness of a solitary Sunday
Wrapped in a duvet in an empty house.

MIKE DI PLACIDO
Losing It
Interschool Cross Country, Scarborough, 1969

If it was just about style and technique
you wouldn't have heard of Paula Radcliffe.
More a quality of will? Which is what failed me
after burning them off through Raincliffe Woods.
Mine to lose – which I did. Not in some
delirium of noise – a lung-bursting scrap
for the tape – but on that quiet country road.
Him: emerging from the trees to become
a drumming presence. Mea culpa ...

Fifty years on and I'm tortured still.
So I offer this poem in part-penance
to the running gods. And if I still went
to church I'd be in the confessional:
'Bless me Father for I have sinned.'

VICTORIA GATEHOUSE
Eight Hundred Metres

On the edge of her shadow
that first lap, the sleek

flick of her ponytail
just beyond reach

as she takes the bend.
We're out in front, kicking

up chalk, she in her Nikes
me in second-hand spikes.

She's a high-street-cred girl,
used to lifting

two fingers as she passes
during cross country runs.

She doesn't know I've turned
feral, goaded

by Revlon-reek sweat, the fear
that's slicked up her skin

as I close in, my breath
hounding her right cheek.

Shoulder to shoulder
we face the home straight

and now, a gasped-out sob
let me win, please

and maybe if I did
I'd be one of her crowd

but it has me by the throat
this need to leave her

doubled-over, six yards back
as I cross the line.

CAROLE BROMLEY

Sprint

I'm eleven though from my height
you might take me for thirteen,
wearing regulation navy-blue knickers
over my white 'linings';
how they hamper me, hand-me-down baggy,
tucked-up like a kid in a story book
fishing for tiddlers; cast-off Aertex shirt
turned dirty grey by the twin tub,
so shrunk it doesn't reach my waist.
I'm sporting a green band for Wenlock
but I'm not running for Wenlock.

I'm running for *me*. I'm running
for the joy of these long feet they tease me about.
Topper they call me because when I grow up
I want to be a Television Topper on the Band Show
and kick my long legs high in defiance
of Hawkeye who mocks my short 'a's,
who says when I move south people will *larf*.
I'm running. In my head I'm seeing how fast
I can thunder my feet on the track.
I'm running. The hundred yard dash
will be mine and no-one will laugh.

VERITY OCKENDEN
Battle Cry

Climb as high
as the rising sun
till you bust your lungs
like bubblegum

Feel your pulse
bring tsunamis
driving your blood
into tangled trees

With ballooning heart
stuck to the sky
let each breath
be your battle cry

STEPHEN LIGHTBOWN
Hitting the Berlin Wall

I sat next to a TV strongman once.
We compared hand callouses,
his from barbells
mine from push-rims.

I watched him last New Year on Channel 5 pull a fire engine towards him
thighs bulging like two deer heads in his shorts
calloused hand over calloused hand
arms burning with expended energy.

I pull on this memory as I lasso a rope around Brandenburg Gate
and drag it towards me.
Mile 26. 200 yards left to go.
Berlin is a mesh of encouragement I don't understand.

About ten minutes ago I'm pretty sure I had a conversation
with an Alsatian holding a sign
padding paw against paw with a *come on, you can do it* furry clap.

Memories of the dog get diluted in the Lucozade I drain.
Did I see it put its sign down and run alongside me?
Los! Schneller! Los! Schneller! Los! Schneller!
Los! Schneller! Los! Schneller! Los! Schneller!
Maybe it was just barking.
I don't speak German or dog.

I tell myself when I get home
I'll look up what was being shouted. I'm distracting myself.
I need to focus on finishing this race.
Breath, push, breath, push, breath, push.

In England I am a wheelchair racer.
Here I am Rollstuhlfahrer.
I like how that sounds.
I repeat it over these last few bits of tarmac:

Rollstuhlfahrer.
Rollstuhlfahrer.
Rollstuhlfahrer.
Rollstuhlfahrer.

Finish line. Banana.

ELISABETH SENNITT CLOUGH

Parkrun

When the runner in his high-vis vest
shouts *get out of my fucking way*
during the first two hundred metres
of a Christmas Day parkrun,
I'd love to be able to say it made me run
faster – that I thought of Liz, Paula or Kelly,
maybe even Kathy Switzer at Boston
in her bulky Sixties tracksuit, out-dodging
the official as he fumbled for her number
to disqualify her: *get the hell out of my race* –
instead, I slow down, my skin redder
(what is the precise body temperature
at which your emotions reach boiling point
but you keep them tightly wound within?),
as I tell myself he's right: what jaded
forty-four-year-old mother-of-three
could call herself a *runner* at this pace,
my state of mind must surely be nothing less
than a series of cul-de-sac ambitions
when my lung-function is worse
than a pair of perforated bellows,
and my eyes panicked as an alarmed deer –
how dare I get in the way of a *fast man*
and not move to the side when he shouts at me,
then look for a side-road exit
to discreetly take myself out of the park,
the house of my body in such a state
of dereliction that the voice inside resounds
so loud against all the emptiness, louder
than anyone on the outside could be,
when I remind myself to run
and not *get in my own fucking way*.

RIVER WOLTON

Run

There's virtue in the air, I sniff it,
snap my eyes awake; called to running
by the lack of traffic noise,
the Sunday shape.

An instant of regret is quickly lost,
I don't linger in the kitchen door
or frame myself lulled with eggs
and beans, a wodge of papers on the floor.

Keys dropped behind an oil-can in the porch
I break spider webs, open the door,
rubber soles meet gravel, skirting
last night's slugs, the rim of path.

There are stages; start with falling forward,
select the less cambered street,
find the rhythm of the now, shoulders
edge the line of dance in sweeps.

Downhill at first towards the yellow gritbox,
wind will be friend, I simply craft gravity
and impact, recipe
of stone and flesh.

Round the corner, don't look at the road
curve up beside the terraces,
breathing measured,
climbing the quiet morning's rope,

tempting myself with just a little more –
the world's prizes are waiting at the top,
I choose and choose with each slap of my hundred bony feet,
don't stop, don't stop.

LYNNE REES

I am running through the wondrous silence of history

past standing stones, invisible tombs, the path Chaucer's pilgrims took across the North Downs, the stone cold dead in churchyards, listening to the sound my feet make on lanes, on mud and stone, sharing my breath, the thump of my heartbeats, with sheep, the sky, fields. Sometimes I wonder how I got here, what propelled me forward to this moment when the snags of fleece along a wire fence shine with glory, when another rise in the track ahead is an inspiration not a defeat. And I think of the words, 'yes', and, 'you can', and the centuries of people before me who said them out loud, or quietly to themselves, believing that something could change. And here I am changing almost nothing in the world and still feeling better for it.

trail run
seeing the wood
and the trees

JOHN GOODBY

The Tough of the Track: an Alf Tupper triptych
I

You kipped in the scullery of Aunt Meg's back-to-back
down Anchor Alley; but when she tried to thieve
your last half dollar from the tea-caddy, it was time to take
up your striped mattress and walk. Slowly, the house fire,
orphanage, Mudd Lane Secondary, a trade – plumber
was it, or welder? – revealed themselves.
                                    Though as salt
of the earth, you never spilt these; seethed more at the smaller
injustices that define a green indignation at the world.
That sack of kittens, say, about to be flung in the cut
by some yob, the sobbing kid whose bike has just been pinched.
At these your purer cause would jut its jaw, and dash

heedless between swerving cars, scarved housewives' heads
turning, an applecart upended, police-whistles shrilling
as you collared him. Or solitary returned, with honest head-
scratchings; an instinct flummoxed, yet true.

                                    Grateful tears
are brushed off with gruff kindness; rewards underwrite
your natural order – a casual fiver, a fish-and-chip supper
from Sam Kessick's caff, annuls all wrong; setting the world right
is all in a day's work. So, goggled, gloved, boiler-suited, stern-
grinning, your pride was the torch's acetylene tongue,
fiercely violet in the dark arch of a viaduct, a life of labour
welded flush to a life of running, to our running life.

II

This grubby singlet / scrunching the cinders
past gasometer / towpath / twice round the Rec
still breathing steadily / feels pain absorb
it / visible cold the plumes / loner alone
paced Greystone Dogs' hare / one floodlit evening
to thank a good pal / to scorn any charity
liberal newfangledness / you subaltern-freckled
biff Vic Mason proper / 'Tupper, you guttersnipe!'
as dressed down by blazers / with 'Bloomin' Ada!'
crash a holdall of wrenches / on changing-room tiles
AAA toffs wince / blench / amateurs aghast
'Cor!' / no brylcream no pack-drill / or escape
either / love death on those lines / is poetry
grooved by such lanes / in the track's blancoed zero.

III

Truculent uncomplaining underdog, a have-a-go hero,
he hoes the row of reconciliation to the world, and to

inequity; unless gall and class unhinge at underdoggedness
at guileless, blithe outrage. As they never do, however

you graft, bristled hair irrepressible, eager-faced, changeless
to move on. Only dreams coincide, or rhyme in some final

frame, where we also run, also-rans returning dead-beat
from the out-of-town no-job, lone passengers on the milk train,

sleepless, frozen. The day of the Big Race! And we must
doze off too, slumped on the top deck of the bus: miss our stop,

panic, clatter off, dash back towards White City's towers,
frantic to draw level with our lives. And so arrive always

breathless, sprinting to the Steward's table with a chit,
whipping on spikes, plunging into the great bowl's roar

having given the field a good fifty yards. From the crowd
a bubbled yell of 'You can do it Alf!', and the rejoinder

'Not a hope, chum!' But reel them in he will, as we will
him on, as the newshounds gape in disbelief, the sour-faced

enemy swears, as he tucks in, Tough of the Track, behind
Cliff Willoughby, 'Flapper' Farmer and Skimba Ru; to take

the bell, bloody-minded as comeuppance – still the one-man
Tristan da Cunha team (or, blistered, blind for months, eyes

bandaged, leaping the water-jump by touch) – to dive, breast
the tape at the very last, smile-crying gasp 'I ran 'em all!'

MARK FIDDES

Lane Discipline

i.m. Margaret Fiddes 1933-2017 and Roger Bannister 1929-2018

She fell for a lover of miles,
for his heron-legged stride,
how he flopped across the line
in three minutes fifty nine,
how Iffley Road dissolved
in flash bulbs and light rain
before they raised him up
by his pale, naked shoulders
like the Jesus Christ of Speed
on the Scala screen in Paisley.
There could be no 2nd Coming;
even with all the Kennedys,
the Georgie Bests and Borgs,
none ran her heart so close
to beating a world record
although they never spoke.
"He's a neuroscientist now,"
she said in the bumpy Uber
back from her brain scan,
as if it might have helped
either, so Britishly together,
in separate lanes at the tape.

MARK GRANIER

Stopwatch

Over fifty now, one of those joggers who pass,
heads down – hard shins and soft knees – eyes on the grass,

I crank myself into old age, hold to the thin
muddied track made by runners, that keeps grass down.

Here I come, round and around, the tip of a second-hand
on a blank green clock, marking what will unwind

lap by lap, the lagging flesh on its beat
from what will escape it: spirited, hard-soled, fleet.

BARRY TENCH

Cross Country

and all I knew was that you had to run, run, run without knowing why you
were running – Alan Sillitoe, 'The Loneliness of The Long-Distance Runner'

The changing room smarts with old sweat and Deep Heat
the stink of dried-in socks and I'm bent-over mud-hard
laces, at the back to be forgotten, to run-out unnoticed

for those blood warming sprints downhill, in rain-cold
in frost-crisp, in snow-melt, over sports field, over tracks
to iron gates, to school, past work-day streets that hold

the run, through the burn, through the sharp-wet valleys
but never to fall, to fall is to fail, to fail, to be flayed
with knotted-towel, with old defeat ringing in your ears.

This new pack run-bright in Lycra, check, pulse, check
as they exit the park, turning my energy to stone-muscle
as runners run past in Nike-winged victory to lap-sprint

while I, in thin vest and thin pumps, run opposed, stark
in the sting of urine tears on red-sore legs, over the hard
pavement-smack, the down-slide of muddy embankment

nothing noble here, no cheering crowd, no winning line
for me to break; just the queue to stand against cold tiles
to watch the spinning mud-brown waters drain in the steam

to find in the mirror my mud-brown hair, fat-fingered face
then unbuttoned miss the bus, take the cinder path, count
my steps, the rhythm-walk to home, freedom the singular race.

DUNCAN CHAMBERS
Thornes Park, Wakefield

We need more words for mud:
the black quagmire that sucks off your shoes,
the brown slick whipping your feet
from under you; the plaster
that congeals on your calves,
comes off in lumps and blocks the shower.

We'll see them all today, along with roots
stretched out like tripwires, stray dogs,
an asphalt path to blunt the spikes
and jar the pelvis. Five laps to run,
five times the long climb through the trees
and not a hope of winning.

We change in a tent that smells of damp
and shudders in the wind. The club vest
clammy on your skin, your number
never straight. We wish each other
a good run, not luck. Time to warm up,
somebody says, and laughs.

Afterwards, flapjacks, bananas,
the football scores, your heart
still beating hallelujah. The glow
of lights at junctions, traffic signs.
Tomorrow you will see your name
in the results, the annals of the blessed.

PETER SANSOM

Cross Country

You didn't ask anything of me, just head-down ahead
Of the tortoise, somewhere in the first forty
The sport of also-rans, I never stepped
From the crease to find the boundary
And the winner hammered home in the last gasp of extra time
That wasn't me, that wasn't mine
I slept your miles
A number pinned to my chest
You weren't exciting though you hurt
You had no rules to stay alert for
You were a lifestyle along the byways
Of couch grass and abandoned railways
And every day was training
Dumble Woods, bluebell woods and the dripping
Ploughed field in between,
Every day was training
Even the dog said give it a rest
Drizzle in the desert of fresher's week
You were meek and not sexy
Though you were your own purpose
You were midweek even on Saturday
When we got off the coach in Derby
Not the cinder tracks of Helsinki
With no thought of winning
We lined up at the back and stayed there

In our own beginning
I ran through those days like water
Through mud
I ran with a little song in my heart for years
And my heart in my ears
The earth went round the sun
The earth went round the sun
And I went after it

'against the rising light'

PINDAR, TRANSLATED BY FRANK NISETICH

from Olympian XI (*Pindar's Victory Songs*)

Sometimes men need the winds most,
 at other times
  waters from the sky,
   rain descendants of the cloud.
   And when a man has triumphed
  and put his toil behind,
 it is time for melodious song
to arise, laying
  the foundation of future glory,
a sworn pledge securing proud success.

For Olympian victors, such acclaim
 is laid in store
  without limit, and I
  am eager to tend it with my song.

JAN HERITAGE

Yes Tor Hill Race

This might be a good place to pitch
your blue tent, somewhere on fairly level ground
with minimal thistles, few stones
and well away from that leat's rush.

I'll peg the groundsheet, keeping it taut
against the push of grass and crowberry.
I'm swift with pole and guy, will turn the whole
away from prevailing wind, the footpath

and any risk of greetings. I crawl inside
this nylon skin, quietening breath and pulse
to better overhear the clack of gorse
some metres away, and the work

of ground beetles, much closer.
Ear pressed to moor, I listen for reverberations
in the peat, try to imagine your footfall
heading northwards along the ridge.

ERIC CHANDLER

20180611
Sacramento
4 miles

I went out into the heat and ran down the sidewalk under the Sewing
Machine sign that marked a closed repair shop but there was a homeless
guy underneath with skin so brown it was almost black from the sun
and I kept going over the train tracks so modern and shiny and over the
black spots from the spat out gum and past the guy in the tunnel who was
busking playing drums and as I came out of the tunnel a police car drove
down into what was a pedestrian way, I thought, and when I came back
later there was no drummer, to the river past the touristy shops and Old
Sacramento and downstream along the Sacramento River when I normally
go upstream. More homeless people. So hot in the pavement sun along the
railroad tracks.

I normally go
upstream, but I wanted to
follow the river.

HELEN MORT

Fox Miles

Supple as a dream I can't call back,
a vixen, in the hedgerow's
matted black, is startled out
to skirt the dawn, and vanish with the dark –
her flame-bright tail extinguished
by the railings of the park. But first,
she bolts across an empty road
and keeps her pace with mine. I slow
to look at her across the gap. We run in time.

She turns her face. Her eyes flare
in the artificial light, and then
she finds a trapdoor in the night;
a corridor towards the sun that she
slinks down alone, and covers miles
she might mistake for home.
And what she sees she cannot tell,
but what she knows of distances,
and doesn't say, I know as well.

LAURA MCKEE

Alnitak, Alnilam and Mintaka

Three yellow balls on a riverbank,
in a perfect representation of Orion's Belt
fallen to earth.

Because of course those stars are far away,
and would be football sized at least here.
This moment just across the river from me,

my gift from the heavens to stop running,
lean on some railings,
be breathless with wonder, instead of asthma.

At how I am even moving this fast at my size,
with my significantly scarred lungs.
At how did the stars get here.

LIZ LEFROY
Running Advice

On hearing I've taken up running, my brother mentions fish oil
like it's the next most logical thing in the conversation.
We're on the telephone because he's one of the few people
I talk to on the phone any more, and it's a Saturday morning.
I'd just got back from my run when it rang, and it was him.
It's on account of us not being young any more, he says.
We need to take care of our joints. I reply that I was always
four years younger than him, which he acknowledges.
Younger is how I feel after completing circuits of the park
in the early light, with the air clear and cool, and my blood moving.
I tease him, ask whether I'm to apply the oil externally.
Of course not, he states, sounding on the verge being a doctor.
Which he is, he's a cardiologist, and a good one at that,
and I can tell that on this matter he expects to be taken seriously.
While we're talking, I'm looking out of my upstairs window
at the people going about their business in the street below.
The sun is showing up the dirt on the glass and I notice
that after my run I have the energy to consider cleaning windows.
This is what I am thinking about when he asks about footwear.
I look down at my old trainers. I'd got in from my run
and only just put on the kettle and not yet had time to mix
the pancake batter or squeeze oranges when the phone rang.
For goodness sake, my brother says, when he hears my silence,
buy some decent trainers. You need to take care of your knees –

and try not to run on hard surfaces. I decide not to tell him
about the tarmac path by the river through the avenue of lime trees.
The orange sun was still low in the sky at half-past eight,
and it was hard to look directly at the swans taking off midstream.
I can hear him thinking, because the line is clear as a bell,
and he's working out how much to write on the cheque
that he will send me for my birthday in three weeks' time.
I've got to go in a minute because I haven't showered yet, I say,
and I'm getting fragrant. There's nothing like a shower followed by
breakfast after an early run, he says. And on this we agree.
Well, good to talk and thanks for the advice, I say.
Just one more thing, he says. Never look down.
When you're running, look up, and always look ahead.

OLIVER COMINS

Jogging

His breathing deepens, starting a first circuit
after stretching, then settles into two-stroke
rhythm with each stride. No-one else hears
those creaking joints roll and ease in oily air.

All the English trees are silent now, holding
their own counsel, trying not to catch his eye,
but the Eucalyptus beside the bowling green
waves its sociable leaves every time he passes.

JANE ASPINALL

10k

Just as autumn gave way to winter
As the leaves fell open and lifted
Like momentary magic carpets,
Along the lines of hedges and verges
Past closed gates and badly fenced fields
Over pavements and cinder paths we ran.
Weightless, the pea in the whistle,
Under sky and street lights and always
The night air hovered like a promise
And left its metal on our lips.

We ran though nobody came or went
And the trees and night birds made no comment
And the only sound was our feet in the road
That seemed to make the earth move.
Indoors, people ate, checked their mail,
flicked channels, made love or slept
and all the while you were with me
counting out the rhythm on the hills.

STUART PICKFORD

Hill

Des Grands Causses

Mist below in the valley, you tempt me
with my Brocken spectre for company.

All week, you've been trying to get inside
my head. Stiff knees tell me I've started.

My way is a mark on your flank. Soon
the taste of blood, coughing phlegm.

For a second, a stonehenge on the horizon.
I look again – four motionless horses;

across their black eyes, something stirs.
There's yesterday's path, beside the well.

No wish, just your abyss staring back
and a cracked stone trough, bone dry.

Monday, the low sun showed me
the spiders' hammocks in the brambles.

Quick-footing over roots, I tripped,
nailed the word *bastard* to the ground.

Friday, I got lost looking for a tumulus,
thought the only way to go was back.

Today, collecting your miles, I emerge
from the high woods, turn for home

when a plum drops at my feet. I stop,
eat. Through its sweetness, I take in

what you've given: the bony outcrops,
curved fields – and somewhere the horses.

NIALL CAMPBELL
A New Father Thinks About Those Running Home

All told, there wasn't much I understood
about this need to run. The first steps on
the pavement like a knocking at a wall –

then the ears tuning out so that the rest
is just a silent picture show: the drivers
with their last deliveries gliding cages

to the light of shop-doors. The night race,
the dark streets humdrum and beautiful.
I had a dream of running, this was it:

long straights, long hills – until a friend described
how if there's a true art to any of it
it happens on the route home, when the streetlamps

are all giving-in above his head –
then, the good runner is just a heart doing
what it's told – *beat, just beat* – and a pair of lungs

trusting they are on fire for the right goal.
Here, up since early, comforting my child,
I have not run – but long to be the runner

if only to gift myself those same commands.
I am so tired, so tired, so young – *Heart, keep on*;
the air's so still – *Lungs, burn hard, burn long.*

ALAN BUCKLEY

Run

for Helen

You catch a dozing whippet unawares.
It startles, offers back an anxious stare,
all jittered by its big, arrhythmic heart
from which it pleads forgiveness for some hurt
it's caused you, although it's done nothing wrong.
It whines like a bruised child however long
you try to soothe it, totters at your heel
from room to room, until you start to feel
frustrated. Wait. Don't judge its temperament.
You've not yet seen it in its element.

Ears cocked. The bushes rustle. Over there –
a twitch of squirrel; look, a zig-zag hare,
though they're not goals, just framework for the race.
That huge heart settles as it picks up pace.
Driven, for sure, but not by hunger, fright
or even rage, and though it's in your sight –
this black bolt through the meadow – still, you know:
its running takes it somewhere you can't go.
Ahead is Silver How. By Langdale Beck
its body sleeks and blurs, can't be called back.

NATALIE WHITTAKER

The ring-necked parakeets
of South East London

are screaming and green;
in their hundreds they lift

from fired-up trees
and flee over luminous joggers,

reined lurchers, a lake,
into a highlighter-pink sky,

as beyond park gates, rudeboys rev
their snarling engines.

And if night starts anywhere, it's here:
the earth leaching light from the sky

as the sun's dusty projector bulb dies.
We splash through dark that pools on paths

and run from the evening that roosts,
silencing the suburbs.

PAUL STEPHENSON

The Result is What You See Today

Rydal, Lake District, Cumbria

1

The valley is open
daily for light,
shuts early if dim,
late when bright.

2

By the mill
water takes its toll;
between far and few
spills the waterfall.

3

In view of the beck,
time, decay, neglect;
each foot of the flight,
a moss-kissed step.

4

The tree is a relic,
that oldest chestnut;
run rings around age,
bark back!

5

Question the quarry,
stand up for stone;
on the upper path,
keep slant till home.

IGOR KLIKOVAC, TRANSLATED BY JOHN MCAULIFFE

Gratitude to Big Cities

Those days when all pages are empty
are best given to running. Knowing your own name
is less important if the streets are long, and – better still –
freshly scrubbed by rain. Then it looks
like you're jumping from one façade to another,
across the outstretched necks and open windows. That alone
already feels like an improvement. Under coloured canopies,
through the courtyards of tiny churches, over pedestrian bridges
that cross no water, through the sleepy eyes of rear-mirrors,
from shop-window to shop-window, like a rambling thought.
Underneath you, the specially designed soles squeal,
and manhole covers rattle with the rhythm of images
barely catching up with their own mortality statistics ...
The problem of the cracked self, thus reduced to a simple
breathing exercise, at the end simply solves itself, like
a common cold. When finally you open your eyes,
the world is again joined up by words, the light thread
which meanders through the scenery like yellow stitching
in a pair of blue-jeans, and the woman taking a jumper
from a washing-line and smelling it, while behind her
in the distance a weather balloon rises, is already
surrounded by that insatiable whiteness, the one
which never lets out what it once swallowed.

MARK CONNORS

On the tops

Sunday. The road through Slippery Ford all yours
and you produce the only sounds you hear:
each breath in sync with slap of running shoes.
Behind a boundary wall, a slow hare

bounds silent, parallel, disappears in heath
of moor, as if it was never there.
Perhaps it wasn't. You rarely trust yourself
with apparitions. They are everywhere

on the tops, some living, some dead. A grouse
appears, without so much as a chortle,
at ease on asphalt. Despite the stillness,
there *is* danger. You are easy kills

below brow of hill. You don't know what's coming.
You stop. Grouse tilts his head, waiting for *this*
to seem real. Even the wind is missing;
this higher plane of living now on pause.

But a kestrel undoes everything.
It halts into a hover. Grouse scarpers,
up the brow and over. How can all this happen
just for you? And then, a sudden shower

sets you off again. In a field, ahead,
a curlew shrieks a version of its name,
as if to warn itself *you are* a threat.
If you could see yourself on this empty lane,

your manic grin, your awkward breathing,
not even close to being dressed for this rain,
you might emit a *curl-lee* too. The wind
returns, shoves each breath back down your throat. Pain

reminds you trails go easier on the knees.
You stop for a rest at Pepper Pot Farm.
A kitchen window frames a worried face.
You smile to let her know you mean no harm.

You just can't help looking in. A radio
is talking. She's washing pots, her eyes on you,
aware of what is going on below
via news, news you would rather not know

right now, so you refrain from trying
to pick out words in fresh elemental din.
You hear grouse laughing, a kestrel shrilling.
A sky frowned with colours moves you on.

HELEN MORT
Coffin Path

Who'd jog along the Coffin Path?
Most evenings only me,
hurrying between

the huddled trees,
boulders streaked with rain,
the bowed heads of the ferns,

on stones worn treacherous
by centuries – men shouldering
the dead from Ambleside.

Today, the dark's grown courteous:
shadows seem to step aside
to let me pass,

just like that summer afternoon
in Cambridge, when a hearse
gave way to me near Jesus Lane

and I sprinted on, noting the driver,
black-capped, glanced at his watch,
certain he'd overtake before too long.

GEOFF COX

Early Start, Winter Run. impression sequence

Set my watch running, check my gloves and hat
leave the silent kitchen and a hearth-warm cat.
Sky bold with stars, ground iron-hard
a spilt-sugar crackle on the hoar frost yard.

Set an easy pace through the first two miles
to the frost-etched woodgrain of the field-gate stile.
Sheep eyes glitter in my headlamp beam
a thin mist rising from the half-iced stream.

There's pale light spilling through a lambing shed door
the soft sound of music and the sweet scent of straw.
A shaded-bulb shining in the farmhouse porch
farm-boots standing ready with a waiting torch.

Rubbing ice crystals from a tear-rimmed eye
breath coming faster up the first real rise.
Weave through the gorse-clumps on the frontside ridge
the only real option since floods took our bridge.

Slow the pace and focus as the limestone starts to show
blunt toothy outcrops, dull-grey against the snow.
Touch the summit pillar then pause to take the view
a hard-set winter valley and a silver setting moon.

Time to turn for home now, time to start my day
commuter headlights snaking down the distant motorway.
Steady down the steep stuff, hop and step and slide
holding breath and trusting studs, holding arms out wide.

Slowing through the ginnel, then a cold seat on the step
to wrestle frozen laces in a crystal cloud of breath.
Throw my steaming trainers in the boiler room
set the kettle on the stove for a breakfast brew.

ALWYN MARRIAGE
Morning Run

It's 8 o'clock: I'm out enjoying
the clear calm golden morning air.
But where are all the horseflies
that plagued my walk last night?
Presumably they're all still fast asleep
deep down in their straw or dung,
digesting those delicious portions of
my knee, my elbow and the left side
of my neck.

RACHAEL MEAD
The dog, the blackbird and the anxious mind

The dog sleeps on the couch as if he's crash-landed.
Cold light from ABC Breakfast is bluing the walls
and I'm antsy as the blackbird beyond the window
fossicking the same ground over and over, the shadows
and the leaf litter, where no-one else wants to look.

The dog and I both need to be run. He drags me
as if I'm emotional baggage he's desperate to escape.
We are linked by more than the lead, more than
the family of mammals, the family of pasts we want
to forget. Both of us are rescued creatures.

And while I know it's a mistake to confuse kinship
with intimacy, my mind shies from the thought that
he stands ahead of me in the long queue for the grave.
My feet spin the earth like a treadmill until my blood
does its rich work and I start to see the world again

as more than a cold pebble hurtling through space
pursuing its own adventures. Everything is standing up,
brimming with its own life and like the blackbird,
I can't leave it alone, going over and over this world,
looking out through eyes ringed with gold.

SUZANNE CONWAY

Coach

All winter we drove to Forches Cross:
the wind pushed on the car doors
and clothes sailed as we peeled off layers.

The fields were black and edgeless
but we didn't care. You tucked the key
behind the wheel and off we sprinted

into dark, hail racketing
anoraks, pelting skin. At the time
I never thought about anything else,

too busy leaping puddles,
resisting gravity, quick-stepping
to more solid ground.

I remember how quietly I loved
the rhythm of your footfall,
your snakes of breath carried off

by the gusts tangled and hissing
in the trees, blowing through Eden.

RAE HOWELLS
School Run

You gave me your camellia flower, bright as a shepherd's warning.
It filled your outstretched palms, its gorgeous mouth open.
You put it on my flat palm and told me, be careful mamma.
I left you at the school gates and ran home, balancing.
The flower funnelled rainwater onto my hand, clear, gluey.
I passed the camellia bush, bleeding its flowers on the pavement.
Yesterday it had been a yellow snail shell, curled foetal.
As a girl, I walked this way from school, past gardens, to my
                                    grandparents' house.
Pavements cannot love, but they can catch your falling feet.
Camellias are symbolic of the divine, of children, of longevity.
Every day you take such a long time to walk up the hill into the winter sun.
This road is rooted in us; you shrub your way up into girlhood.
Every worm, every flower, a pause. My hands are wet, running, honeyed.

DIANE MULHOLLAND

The Ultra Runner

God adds a small stone to the summit cairn,
takes in the Colorado view, then turns
to head back down. He takes it easy,
checking out the wildflowers one side,
an empty rattlesnake skin on the other
as his sneakers mark the trail, raising puffs of dust.

It's tough up there, the heat can make you
see things in odd ways. The work is in the mind
as much as heart and muscle. I like to think
that when he gets back down to where his crew
is waiting that he high-fives them all in turn
before dropping forwards, hands on thighs, chest heaving.

BETH MCDONOUGH

Tempting the Runner Off the Green Circular, Dundee

Notice how this bit of the Dighty slows,
at the cycle path's slit through unkempt parks.
A low water flow of drag-down plants
flags sufficient green to throttle Ophelia.

Brambles September this morning.
Pass beech, wind turbines and black rose hips.
An invitation, silver-sharpied
on the dog-waste bin, suggests you ditch your knickers.

Unseen, ahead, and as yet unheard
some grim reaper clears the margins and his throat.
You scent the fresh death of seeding bishop weed.
Deep Heat and bent-necked comfrey heal to the fore.

Himalayan balsam invaders, which you know
you shouldn't like, now begin to pick out in pink.
In the shallows, two upturned ASDA trolleys
offer sunk possibilities. And too much fun.

NELL FARRELL

Blessing at the Allotments

I'm the one dressed for a ritual
running shoes, iPod looped through my fleece,
mouthing the smoky prayer of a soul song.

She's simply walking the muddy paths
hands in her pockets. The third time we cross,
something arcs between us

we break off and smile, talk sunshine,
bird song, ramshackle sheds.
Then she says *I come here to say my rosary.*

I run on with something bestowed
imagining *Hail Holy Queen*
rising up through the trees

with the midges and the bonfires
and the broken notes
escaping from my headphones.

LIZZY TURNER

trajectory

I get an idea of how far he can go when I watch him   he's away
before I know what's happened   black hair on shock yellow,
nearly vanishing streetlamp to streetlamp   vespid   knowing to
leave for the dark   and he gets so far so quickly   without the
warning dot of his jacket I wouldn't see where   and who could
ever keep up with him   let alone me   I watch him tear off
(more likely away-from than to, which is better)   and it's okay,
just beautifully sad to see him out there   never knowing what
is out there with him, what his eyes look like   from here his
form is perfect but he keeps on going   and perhaps I don't
worry because when he runs in a ring there is a return to the
beginning and I have always found him waiting for me   and he
can only keep coming back if he keeps going   but I know that
he knows where the edge is   and luckily he knows much better
than me (because I can't see what is out there with him)   how
much or little effort it would be to take that one skip and hop
out of my sight

DIANA MOEN PRITCHARD

Forest Run

Fall and a sprinkling of snow.

Jogging along a logging track
through the darkening timber
of lodge-pole pine and Sitka spruce
balancing on the edges of ruts
frozen ridges of churned mud
fleeing a teenage angst
desiring aloneness
respite from filial demands

paternal clutches
I came upon a clearing.

By a pile of sawn logs
ageing under the heavy light of snow-cloud
I stopped to listen to the silence
to feel the stillness
to breathe the freedom.

Then, out from the camouflaging background
of the woodpile, like an apparition,
a lynx appeared, tufted ears alert
still as a sphinx.

We observed each other for an eon
as something passed between us
some recognition
something other than fear
some affinity with our shared wilderness.

We turned away in unison.
She, to slink back into the forest,
me, hair bristling down my neck,
to run for home.

JONATHAN MAYMAN

phantom runner

when walking down to the village today
behind me heard a sharp pitter-patter
turned round ready to get out of the way

as I half-expected no-one was there
during sleep he causes my brain to fuse
high-stepping through a recurrent nightmare
ever since I hung up my running shoes

STUART PICKFORD

Running Against Wordsworth

Soon the body quietens and the heart
spreads its heat. Fells are turning
their best side to the sun when he drops in
on my shoulder, his first Windermere.

He's got all the gear. Top of the range
reflector shades. We bound around
a bit like deer. In dizzy rapture,
the living air diffuses in our lungs.

But the horizon uprears its craggy head,
the aching joy transforms to aching,
corporeal. I inform Will our hearts
are pumping six gallons per minute.

His reply – *time and the hour run
through the roughest day* – has no legs.
At the next drinks station, he slumps
in blank recollection by the gloomy wood.

I push through caverns of pain, shorts
stained with crusts of salt, my shirt
cling-film. The path ahead messes about
in heat haze. The big views die.

The way to make it stop is to keep going:
cramp grabs calves, clenches quads,
feels for my heart; each step pounds
the path, the rocky, bastard path.

LIZZIE HOLDEN
Spring Run

Beat, bum, rubber hoof, piston fist,
soft mesh feet sprung.
We crush cinnamon curl leaves, kill twigs.
That bud will never open now.
Grass stems bend double,
we don't know if they will recover.
Heron feather splayed, muddied,
we make the worms shudder, rabbits hide,
snails move a little faster.

SARAH PASSINGHAM
In my treads

This one, knobbled and red from the tow-path.
This one, round like a pearl from when the land was covered by sea.
This one, blackened with Tarmacadam and scented
from when they mended the road.
This one, yellow like a viper's eye from that track where the May thorn blooms.
This one is a thorn.
This one, soft, a lump of clay from The Pits behind the pub.
This one, smooth, flat, stuck proud – made my Nike Pegasus steel-heeled.
This one, resists my digit; stuck fast until I squeeze the sole
then it flies with a ping.
This one, silvered, glinting, is not a stone at all; the head of a horseshoe nail left
from when the pasture was ploughed.

WENDY PRATT

Godsong

Lose the trail of prayers that hang
about the head like moths and watch,
instead, the tendon of road swerving
through a bluster of trees.

Birds will fall away, losing their song
to your footfall as you ignite
the leaves as only you can; bleed
into the heat beneath your feet.

Swing to the rhythm; you are sudden
and serene at once. Your heart is a fist,
clenched, remembering what it is
to survive, not just exist.

GILES GOODLAND

The Canal Path

Into half light I run, up to the canal.
When fevers tremble under the surface
the gloss on the surface is partial to you.

The heron bends its knee and reconstructs
flight. It doesn't fly so much as use the
air as stair. The starlings dissemble mass
into verb in order to sculpt body.

The woods lengthen, the water corrugates.
By the lock, things rise to their names.

Two strong-winged swans just enough abreast
so that their wings do not brush
leave feather-trails on the water. That rushing
is air's substance,

inebriation of tree into black.
I had not dreamt this far before,
like paired clouds settling in the eye
we'd know already the swans draw with them
the sun and turn it into weather

but the hill itself is no challenge, and the light
just gone, that slant evening
as inside us the dusk travels.

IFOR THOMAS

Autumn Run

I feel the swirl from Irma's skirts
on my clifftop run.

Down on the beach road,
wave dragged shingle
grates the air,
wind tugs my running shirt,

as if there's something there,
something I've missed.

Feet ferret the rabbits' path,
I smell mushrooms
as my fingers
snatch at snot.

Clouds lean in over me,
a squall sweeps the sea.

PAM THOMPSON

Running, Anglesey, Easter

Grey stone, pebble-dashed;
at the front, a drive, three cars.
At the back, a terraced lawn;
a gate; rotting steps, an estuary
which is sometimes a river;
sometimes a stream you can wade across.

The beach is from early childhood –
the first footprints, or rather trainer prints,
in the morning, yours. The sea even smells of sea –
weedy, coconut oiled.

At first there's nothing to scare you.

But then a biker blasts past; teenage boys,
brown chests bared, spring from a dune,
say get off their fucking turf.

Relatives are watching from the safe house –
look up, you can't see them.
Windows are blank grey water.

Now, the river bends.
You are between the sand dunes and the sea.
Now they have lost you.

MATTHEW WEST

Evening Out

Looking out from the steps of Black Sail Pass
it doesn't seem possible to leave the saddle
by Stirrup Crag and land in Wasdale Valley.

Best give it a miss, spur off at Yew Barrow,
take a slow trot along the Horseshoe Ridge;
try not to think of torn muscle, broken limbs

or the gravity effect, that hot rush of air
as you hurtle down the chimney breast,
smoke signals pulsing from cross-shoes on scree.

Tighten the aperture and focus on the future,
the smile that won't shift tonight at Ritson's
when the first pint washes sweat from lips

each casual gesture raising a shower of dust
to settle as silence while you answer questions
about how the day's running panned out.

You'll tell how you took the afternoon in your stride,
pacing past Pillar, Haycock and Steeple,
bagging Scoat Fell before the sun slipped down

and what else was there but to take Dore Head –
the easy way home, with light already failing
and thirstiness rising like mist from the fells?

JULIE MELLOR

Ghosts

escaped from their bodies | they run downhill
through the dark | from Hartcliffe and Hillside |
mist clings like breath | the white underbelly of
frosted ground resists their footfalls | turquoise
and pink trainers | headtorch beams | silvery
jitters of light they continually aim for | trailing
their own unique shadows | chasing down the
steep slope | trying to leave | or return | gasping
at their imprisonment | fogged sky easing to
daylight | they are made of Lycra | cutting
through winter | across top field | horse field
| set aside | between rows of kale sweetening
in the hard cold | hurting with the need to
be | uprooted | every morning a threshold |
shattering | as I walk the dog | looping the side
of the stream | Henbrook it says on the map | a
ditch | another boundary | where names are lost |

OLGA DERMOTT-BOND

In Sickness and In Health

The Golden Shovel
Another mudfunked Sunday, singletrack tripping
nine miles through the leafdeep and flat
fall light ... – What Happens in Church, Brent Terry

And I know that if I turn right, and then another
right, I will be carried with morning's mudfunked
smell, clean and cold against my face, along my Sunday
route. Still sleepy across steaming fields, life is a singletrack
for an hour, the day not quite shaken out yet, no doubt tripping
me up down these roads – for there is a certainty that after nine

kilometres comes ten. And I know our week together is lost, miles
ago, its ribs showing, roaming over familiar hills, howling through
evenings of silence between us, and I know I can always feel the
indecision under my hungry skin, under my feet, like leafdamp
sticking to every new resolution I make. And you know. And
no matter what I try to resolve, to promise, my heart is tired, flat
now and forever, in sickness and in health, turning inside out, rise and fall,
and so I know nothing but to run down this same path, against the rising light.

'our bodies gone to our heads'

A E HOUSMAN

To an Athlete Dying Young

The time you won your town the race
We chaired you through the market-place;
Man and boy stood cheering by,
And home we brought you shoulder-high.

Today, the road all runners come,
Shoulder-high we bring you home,
And set you at your threshold down,
Townsman of a stiller town.

Smart lad, to slip betimes away
From fields where glory does not stay,
And early though the laurel grows
It withers quicker than the rose.

Eyes the shady night has shut
Cannot see the record cut,
And silence sounds no worse than cheers
After earth has stopped the ears.

Now you will not swell the rout
Of lads that wore their honours out,
Runners whom renown outran
And the name died before the man.

So set, before its echoes fade,
The fleet foot on the sill of shade,
And hold to the low lintel up
The still-defended challenge-cup.

And round that early-laurelled head
Will flock to gaze the strengthless dead,
And find unwithered on its curls
The garland briefer than a girl's.

RACHEL BOWER

Run for your life

run your body free of small hands
so your body is there to give when you get home,

run without bags, dusk cracking yolk in your hair,
past people walking ghost dogs, pissing gold on trees,

run your body free, past the tawny screeching to her love,

kwikk to his call, kwikk to his call,

run your body free, past the tawny screeching to her love,

past people walking ghost dogs, pissing gold on trees,
run without bags, dusk cracking yolk in your hair,

so your body is there to give when you get home,
run your body free of small hands,

run for your life.

MARA ADAMITZ SCRUPE

On Winning the Marathon at Sixty

As if there were fireflies awake at dawn
As though the bite of frost on grass

On coral if color were fastened to the leaked night
the sneaked light

As if the douceur
as if trepidation wore the bib not the runner

as though the runner rode sweetness in anticipation
as the colors of slate & water & the washing over

of flat river stones smoothed the size & shape
of a Red Hawk tail feather

the blue-gray-black wind catch / my gloves
tucked into my singlet

quick stripping to shorts at the first water stop
as if this journey recalls the end   yet not

& exhaustion is the sweetest of all
my body's immunological betrayals

as though condition / disease / sickliness
is one fewer fugitive   as if to walk   yet not

as if pain is anything/everything
of pleasure   as if illness as if tenderness & toughness

ruthlessness stricken in delicacy
in the doe's white tail flying boundless as if

ransomed by this run to the start line
& color corrals & sweetness of all in the crossing

in the final mile: I want to start again   *right now*
in attenuation / time's compaction   as though a quiff

of air led / barely contained   *I'm lit*
watching the clock at each turn

if in the reach as in the grasp   the enveloping
as though in the use of every muscle bone bit of cracking

cartilage: the floating & rafting on
everything   legs light   up my toes to the end

BEN NORRIS
Big Heart

as much as the feeling I loved the facts
the valves and the tubes
the gases and graphs
the solid reliable rankable graft
this fast is this fast is this fast is this fast
this far is this far is this far
you're here and you're there
and you're first and you're last

but when coach said I had a big heart
I wanted to wring the cliché out of him
throw it like a dance over the ruffled rug of the dumbles
parade it through the mud and miles
the slopes and the roads of my youth
spent dreaming of London
when that was a strange place
2012 when that was the future

it takes longer for big hearts to break
takes longer to lose the heat of old flames

when coach said I had a big heart
I wanted anything but science

but this hard is this hard
is this hard is this hard

ROBERT WALTON

Re-Run

It starts with an elderly woman in a long black dress
        and shiny buckled shoes marching her class out
to the playing-field after Arithmetic. Our commanding officer,
        she calls the warm-up drill as if we're on parade:
twist to the left, now to the right, touch our toes five times
        and stretch our arms high to reach for a cloud.
We take our marks on the line. Nudge for elbow-room.
        Deep breaths, lungs full as scuba-tanks.
Pan to Mrs Jones: a whistle held to her chin,
        she points to a distant tree, warns us not to cut
corners or stop – *There and back. It's good for your brains* –
        and I feel the blood pump from my toes to my crown.

In the seconds that become days of reflection sixty years later,
        we fall into place, silhouettes running towards the edge
of Bryn Hafod school field and the council houses beyond the fence.
        Zoom in on Jimmy Wickham loping out in front.
June and Kenneth, close behind – they'll never last. I'm keeping up
        with David, Mary and Glyn as we kick the fallen leaves
around the tree, and Ian Cannon picks up sticks to throw
        at the gasping kids at the back – we know who they'll be.
Cut to the final thirty yards: thrusting arms and legs
        at every stride, we draw deep and tumble past
our teacher to the grass, face down. My chest heaves and my head burns,
        as now, with the smell of earth, sweat and the brain's fire.

ALAN PAYNE

Sprinter

He won every race he entered;
raised a gloved fist
when crossing the line –
for the wretched of the earth.

Accused of ingratitude
by his headmaster,
he chalked on a wall
by the school gate:

    INGRATITUDE
  IS THE FIRST VIRTUE
   OF REVOLUTION

He might have written a book
on his hero, Thomas Paine,
become an activist,
figured in an Olympic final.

At nineteen, he suffered
an epileptic fit.
On his coffin lay his spikes,
and a copy of *Rights of Man.*

NOEL CONNOR

The Gap

George Rogan hadn't missed many dinners,
half horse half man, already
head and shoulders above the rest of us.
I could never catch him,
in two full seasons of cross country
could never close that agonising gap,
always coming in a distant second.

On those bitter winter afternoons
training on the hill behind the school
my lungs would burst, just trying to keep up
watching him spurt away yet again
and at the end, standing hands on hips
pretending it didn't even hurt.
No talk then of carbing up or rehydration,
well before energy bars and sporty gels
or isotonic drinks carried in your kit.
One County race in Ballyclare ended in the dark,
my fingers too frozen to unpick my muddy laces.

The season's final race was close to home,
on the bleak half flooded Bog Meadows
between the Cemetery and the Sewage Works.
This time I decided to stay by his side
Rogan would be sick of the sight of me,
and matching him stride for stride
we stretched away from all the others,
together, opened up a decent gap.
But halfway round my legs deserted me,
seized and buckled drunkenly,
left me splayed out, face down in the mud.

Slogging back, splattered and disgraced,
in the distance I could see the leaders finish
speeding down the slope towards the tape.

But by the final straight the gap had gone,
Rogan caught and overtaken on the line,
doubled-up and gasping,
shocked at coming second, for the first time.

PAT EDWARDS

Spider

They called me Spider when I ran
between the lines on grassy tracks;
fastest girl in school, I couldn't lose
in my white plimsoll running shoes.

After you died my friend dragged
me out to pound away the grief.
My hips complained, got replaced,
walking hills became more my pace.

Now I am old and the Spider in me
yearns to spin webs on silken tracks;
to confound with my eight good legs,
stopwatch out of life the final dregs.

ANTHONY COSTELLO

Running Pacts

*On Joss Naylor, I have a photo somewhere of him presenting me with the
CVFR veterans prize in 1994. I was 45, and as fit as I'd been in my life. Now
I'm knackered, waiting for two new knees ... – Bob Horne*

Give me five more years of running and I
will settle for that (this is crazily optimistic

given the side-lining knocks: Plantar, Knee,
Hamstring, Groin, Back, Spur, Hip),
give me a year injury-free and I'll show 'em,
give me one Summer running at my peak,
give me a running coach, a regular massage,
a pair of broad shoes & full-length orthotics

What social life? What wife? Who'd settle
for a running conversation & fungal toenails,
the dirt at the base a permanent stain,
weekends ruled by Fell-Running dates:
Tigger Tor, Giant's Tooth, Grin n Bear It, Doctor's Gate ...
the price we pay, a permanent limp, chronic pain,
a mountain rescue case, hypothermia, worse,
dissatisfaction, addiction, obsession, delusion, curse.

STUART HANDYSIDES
The rite of autumn

I perform the preparation rituals
of a willing human sacrifice,
stretching all the joints and muscles
I've ever strained, or think I might
– I find more every time;
anoint with talc, and cream to block
the lovely carcinogenic rays.

It's just 10k, but this year I fear
fear decline, fear whatever hurt my knee
and made me limp and caught me out
improved so slowly

that when it let me run again
I could have wept with thanks
to know my body still repaired itself.

JACK HOUSTON

Sunny September Days

Death turns, runs backwards, bouncing high
with each step while I'm struggling to keep up,
my legs burning. So I stop, hands to knees, waiting

for my breath to return.
It's on days like these that Death feels most vigorous;
the two of us gone for a jog, the sky clear,

the sun beaming down and Death
copying my posture, teasing, talking low
in its gravel voice, telling me I can do this.

A squirrel skips along a tree limb with a nut
or some such, ready to stash it away for winter
and the crows alight on their top branches and Death

pats me on the bum, and then seeing a stray football
escaping from some youngsters' game, Death
bounds over to hoof it back with those strong legs.

Returning, Death skips a little, shows me how easy
it is to bounce from the world, gently coaxes me
to keep running. Says I must keep running.

MIKE FARREN

Running with Simon, 1983

This was before I bought that record:
Leonard Cohen's *Songs of Love and Hate*,
for a joke, "My brother, my killer,
what can I possibly say?"

But we breathed together, me too puffed
to speak, and you – I never knew,
until you said, "You don't mind."
It didn't sound like a question.

I lumbered on as you accelerated
effortlessly and vanished
from my sight.

JULIA FORSTER

Running with Mums

After birth, I'd sit on a rubber ring – the sort
you'd sling out to sea if someone were drowning.
I couldn't walk for three weeks. It was a little victory
the day I waddled to the ironmongers
to buy six safety pins. This, my friends,
is what we're dealing with.

Running, it's two fingers up to female physiology:
we scallop our stomachs into Lycra leggings,
suction our breasts into sports bras –
which are more scaffolding, less lingerie –
we eschew all tints of pink, wear shapeless t-shirts,
then stretch outside The Leis, test our pelvic strength

with time trials up the High Street
and, ignoring the haulage lorry's horn,
we pound the pavement towards Glaspwll
where the climb leaves even the fittest among us breathless.
We pause at the sapling oak where one mum
buried her twin's two maroon placentas.
We never forget how far we've come.

SUZANNE CONWAY

Winter Training

It's so cold my teeth ache
and I'm tense, reluctant
to climb out of my clothes.

I can see your breath disappearing
as you stretch
and jump up and down on your toes.

You say: *If you were a stripper*
by the time you undress
everyone will have gone home.

But tonight it's just us
surging across a field
we can barely see, running

into a wall of wind,
hail tapping our shoulders
like someone wanting attention,

wanting to share a thought,
just as I want to tell you:
these nights

with your strides beside me
are the first time
I've wanted for nothing.

MARK GRANIER

Night Run, Mount Merrion, 1975

for Dominic

That impulse – to strip and sprint
past crowds, across a football pitch, a screen –
would have blown past like any season
of yellowed newsprint

if you hadn't caught in it a flash
of your own impulse, to throw night airs
on our friendship: lit window-squares
on a wooded suburban hill marking our dash

but not one twitching curtain, no one to see
our unrehearsed *Midsummer*: intimate
earth with a different spin on it,
our bodies gone to our heads –

cool grass, twigs, footlights of the city spread
livid, streaking through trees.

JULIE LUMSDEN

DASH

That summer of drought, months
of sad city dust. Then, suddenly

buckets of rain

and Crazy Cal steps out of his shoes,
strips himself of jeans, tee shirt

and runs fast

right to the top of Mansfield Road
for the joy of it.

JON MCLEOD

The Middle Miles

In the surgical brilliance of the opening lap
you were everybody's best boy,
your feet found their patter on the spring
pavements, your short name borne
like a birthday badge, 'You've got this Jon',
'Smash it lad.'

It's the middle miles that tear you down,
there you are a stranger in tight pants
and a hospital vest. You have strayed
into a Sunday morning like an amnesiac
looking for his keys. Dogs eye you
with disgust, car doors open in your face.

You pass a school you once attended,
a park where you broke your leg,
a shuttered factory, a muffled fire
in the allotments beyond the bridge.
You are half-lost on a forest path,
a heron lumbers over, its dim laughter.

JOSIE ALFORD

An Exercise in How to Move On

I find running helps,
it feels like halfway between positive and punishing,

recently the past has been catching up.
I've been pounding the pavements
in unsupportive footwear, telling myself
that sanity lies in a 10-minute mile
that I just can't reach when I've been
smoking the tobacco you left behind,

there's certainly a high after the first 10k;
my body buzzes with the love of it,
but the beers necked in celebration smell of you,

it doesn't last,
I end up blistered,
at night, I tighten and ache,
my hips scream, knees burn, ankles cry,
but my brain finally stops running, lies quiet, and sleeps

which I guess
is all I wanted.

M R PEACOCKE

Running

Once there was running, a spurt of joy
in the feet, some unbidden riot
under the skin. Then there was running,
willed. Now the body's dull as lips
of animals mumbling frozen grass,
and if I say, *Do you remember running?*
It pauses, puzzled. It knows its tasks.
It can't recall.

MARK CARSON

Not running but failing

When I was but a child
My feet were flat, spread wide
And flapped to left and right

My mother took advice
And set me exercise
I did it every night

A box of marbles
One by one I scrabble
Pick up between my toes

Barefoot
And place them in those
Pyrex kitchen bowls.

When I was set to run
'Twas not a bowl of fun
I wasn't fast. I came in last.

LORRAINE MARINER
Tritina for My Hips

All my sadness went into my hips
and my shins could not bear the weight of loss
when I tried again at thirty-eight to run.

I'd sped past boys, left them at a loss,
when I was a child and loved to run,
delighting my dad, always heavy in his hips.

But no teenage boys followed where I ran
so I stopped, assumed a girlish tilt to my hips,
and for ten years they have borne my father's loss –

now my hips, girded by loss, cannot run.

JULIAN BISHOP
Treadmill

running on a treadmill in the gym
someone smiles
on the rubber belt next to me

I notice she's about my age
but quite a few pounds lighter and definitely

more motivated. I glance at her
dashboard
see she's running at 10.4
and I'm only 9.8. This isn't on
and I wonder why

she's so much more driven than me.
I land my hand softly

on the dial
inch it three notches higher
and she does the same. I hit the dial again
starting to perspire

seriously now. I note she's on
10.9
my goodness, why are you doing this
I say

because you're a man,
she replies
you wouldn't have it any other way

LEWIS BUXTON

Fragility

Tenderised meat, hedonists, ambulances run through our veins. **Go for a run.**
In the rain. Smashed ornaments, lives that stop like unfinished sentences,
dog meat, crooked teeth, sensitive skin, hot to the touch, *fuck this is all too
much*, shotguns & attics, chemicals & bad luck at being a boy under the age
of forty-five: what a time to not be alive. **Go for a run**, cartilage of emotion.
Che Guevara, teenage bedroom, phantom limbs & ghostly tendons. Best mate,
best man, sunshine, lonely: sweetheart, darling, doll face, honey. You're sexy.
Can't sleep, bad dreams, night sweats, can't breathe. Get up to wee. Quick
shit, blood wipe, ignore, invulnerability. *Why me?* Toast soldiers, yolk runs
like burst vessels, locked in our own blood cells. *Mate, mate, mate, I'm asking
for help.* Celebrate our art, celibate birds who can't migrate or get hard. Gone
soft. **Go for a run**, cool off, our hearts all rag & bone shops. *Stop, stop, stop, I
want it all to stop.* Toilets with broken locks holding in broken men. Another
round of anger please, cleaved souls, carved smiles, hair gel. Our umbilical
cords are rope. *I ran back from the quietest place on the North Norfolk coast, I
hope, I hope, I hope.* High stress, chef whites, depression ugly as steak knives,
all bruised fruit. If we didn't kill ourselves maybe we'd live as long as our
wives. Don't let our wounds heal: sticks, bones, skin, stones. Missed call. Dead

phone. *I feel so alone*, scar tissue to wipe away the sweat & tears. Bad timing, boys dying, smashed windows, joyriding. Men's bodies are libraries of sadness, reading is for girls and we won't read anything without a male protagonist. **Go for a run**, king or captain, actor or chaplain, a eulogy of men shouting, who all have sheds in their hearts & grief in utility rooms, hide shame in old bank statements, fall apart, pulled tendons, stalled engines, no service stations for the heart. **Go for a run**. Man up. Stand down. Stand up. Man down.

ABEER AMEER

The Runner

Not sure when she hit the wall;
the beginning of unending
unfolds to full halt.

Alone with faces and sounds she knows.
A sea of heads and limbs around her
coloured tops drum lightheaded.

Dry mouth. She's off pace. Weak
with sore calves and quads.
Shoes and legs everywhere.

Her scarf has slipped back,
hair clings to her brow. There is no sound.
She holds her *abaya* in her teeth.

She's lost her right shoe, her left hand.
Sweat drips from her ears, she tastes blood,
feels a limp arm around her neck.

She looks ahead, sees green birds,
faces asleep without breath.
Eyes she looked into moments before –
glazed.

DAVID BORROTT

Hainault Road

On a pavement between fast cars
and a ramshackle hedge,
brambles arching into the path,
I like to palm them as I run past,
not for the pain's distraction
but to gain strength from something living,
a high-five as if they were electric
and the jolt pushes me forward, over weeds,
glass, litter and the tarmac's oblong patches. Two miles
that road speeds away and I am a human body
worrying its limit, the way
the boy-racers floor the gas
on the long straight and watch
the needle rise, seventy, seventy-five,
a squeal of brakes before the roundabout.
The mind is different when the body is in use, not so anxious,
unchained, it floats along like a balloon,
while the feet slap and the arms piston
and the legs run away with themselves.

PAUL HOWARTH

it's when the body is at its most like a machine that the mind is at its least like a machine

so run
  run for the run
    of it
      run for the rhythm
        the binary off/on
        metronome of
         feet on asphalt

feet on grass
on gravel
feet on forest
floor and on
run for the punk
of it
the all i need i already have
of it
run for the hell
of it
run for the rage
not away from but into it
headlong and through
run for the fix
of it
oh yes set free your skinful of bees!
run for the run
of it
do you feel that?
that's your body
doing what your body
was made a body to do
childish perhaps
but then isn't every instinctual act
that involves filling a temple with song?
isn't that the call?
isn't that the message you are running to deliver?

RACHAEL MEAD
Outdoor drum solo

My feet play the skin of the earth like a drum,
beats echo up the flutes of my bones.
This primal dance, known marrow-deep
is pleasure and ache, pitch-perfect yet
felt in every cell like feedback screech.
But forget the body, it's all in the mind,
that grit of teeth and will that keeps
my stride's metronome ticking on,
each second a replica of the last.
Huffing in counterpoint as my feet
spin this shining earth, I shed
the dull skin of a life lived inside.
Drumming my solo to this world
of wild, unholy brilliance – I run.

NICHOLAS MCGAUGHEY
Trainers

These shoes used to wait for feet that climbed mountains
And leapt over streams. Sitting under the fire to dry
Stuffed with newspaper, the laces untied.

Now shelved by stilettos and brogues
They wait for feet that can't climb stairs,
That haven't leapt in twenty years.

TERRY QUINN
to my red tracksuit top

my old faithful friend
rescued from a pile
of worn out kit in the corner
of a college gymnasium
just for the day
but found that you suited me
with your rough cotton
and pocket for keys

keys that I left with Martti
my first girlfriend
so I could run for hours
along the Grand Union
expecting her to be home
not flying back to Finland

but you stayed
even after I spewed down your front
deliciously pushing it too far
over dunes at Great Yarmouth
though nowhere near as sick
as when I ran out on Sarah
just a few weeks later

and you've never stopped giving me space
finding room for my inhaler
desperately needed in Hammersmith
remember that run by the river
bench by bench back to Anna
struggling for breath
which I still do when I think of her

I've changed the names
like they didn't change theirs
which just leaves me and you

with your broken zip
and me with my prolapsed discs
but all things considered
we've had a fine run
don't you think.

ROB WALTON

Spanner Skills

I still have the spike spanner that I used
for those white adidas ones and the blue suede
patricks with the two tiny stripes
oh but they were classy
and the shorter 6mm spikes for the track
and the longer 9mm or 12mm
for the cross country
oh but it was muddy and bloody hard
and the misplaced belief
that if I really tightened them
I'd get through a heat
or count for the team

oh but I knew how to get it to the correct torque
so I'd never lose a spike
and risk imbalance and leaning
and falling and getting in the way
of better runners
oh but they were better runners

oh but I never cross-threaded
and I never needed WD40
and I always chose the right length spikes
for the terrain the track the course the conditions
and oh if only my running had been on a par
with my spike spanner skills

PAUL STEPHENSON
Urban Wildlife

It's not every day
a man stops you
in your tracks

to remove a cricket
from the quiff
of your hair,

nor every day
you thank a man
you've never met,

watch him go on
with his height
and his smile,

no joke or decoy,
clever ruse or scam,
nothing to entrap you;

nature's generosity,
a man on the street,
the stranger's touch.

ANNA WOODFORD

Bedsocks; Willow

for G

After a 10k run and 9 years
of marriage you take my foot
in your hands and ease off one
of my bedsocks like a pair
of knickers here in our warm
living room where we always
are at the end of the day.
I have worn bedsocks
since bed became hard
a couple of years ago,
since sleep became
a fantastical figure
hidden under my side
of the bed or mewling
in the depths of the wardrobe,
since at night I failed
to take flight and started
hanging around the dark
kitchen or hanging off
your neck like a wingless
creature – since all that
got better I have hung on
to the bedsocks, the camomile tea
and the hot water bottle meaning
I may never again travel lightly.

Knowing this you ease off
my bedsock with its foolish
Primark hearts and hold my foot
in your hands and the naked
woman hidden in its sole
carefully stroking her jangling
nerve endings after nine years
of marriage and all that running.

*'I won't stop until I've travelled from
one life to another'*

GEOFFREY HILL

from Watching the Boston Marathon

how
amazing it still is, the awaited name
hailed through our streets, under the pale leafage,
springing from the hierarchies of splendour
and salutation, prodigious messengers
with their own heralds and outriders –
yes, look! the Kenyan runners, look, there they go!
stippled with silver, shaking off the light
garlands of sweat –

MARIA TAYLOR

Woman Running Alone

A woman who follows her own trail
and pounds pavements of unending cities,
past statues of forgotten men, fountains,
sticky sunshine pouring over tower blocks,
past gentrified basement windows
where wives hear the washing-up howl
between their hands, past suits on phones
and panda-eyed women in doorways
with faces that say I know, I know – tell me
about it; these streets where open hands
beg for more than is ever offered,
where someone's kid is a sleeping bag,
where the wolf-whistle becomes the wolf
and love's worn like musk aftershave,
where she forgets who she is: Ms. Keep On,
Ms. Never-going-home, neither running away
nor running toward anyone, wind-sifted,
letting the weather sing through her,

'I won't stop until I've travelled from one life to another'   113

she who is different to her brothers.

The rhythm fills her with flight –
        and her wings,
                what wings she has –

MARIE PAPIER

Run, Boorana, Run ...

*According to historical tradition, a man named Oromo began the lineage of
the Oromo people. His oldest son's name was Boorana.*

I left Oromia as I was
in my tattered jeans
the soiled cotton shirt
I wore in prison

    and ran ...

my son
        screaming in my heart
            mother wailing
                my clan chanting in my breast
                    the sun shining on my back
I ran

ran with the sound
      of our tongues
           the rivers' songs

the roaring
bleeting
howling
the squawking and
snorting
      of our wildlife
          spinning in my head

I fled

    Oromia's massacres
    while my blood relatives
    were waning in prison

I left my country
for a safer place
a duller state
where I run
up and down
its lanes
over the bridges
along the railway lines

I run
as if back to Oromia.

SCOTT PALMIERI

The Ex-Convict Runs a 10k

Where else but here,
somewhere near the start line,
would there be
such kind anonymity?
Nervous laughter
for voluntary pain –
tomorrow's torn bodies –
calves seizing,
hip flexor suffering
through the neighborhoods
he tours, where
running alone
would make this all suspicious
to the cop who now
stops traffic for him.

There is forgiveness
in the shin splint,
grace in the knotted quad,
friendship in the struggling lung,
small applause and cowbells.
Even the children are unafraid,
so he may wave back
in this hour
and every race he can find
until his legs give way,
when he outlasts
everyone who hurts
because of him,
as walls of cheers await
and flags wave him on.

PAM THOMPSON

The Run

The crew of the Shuttle Columbia did not return safely to Earth;
we can pray that all are safely home. – President G W Bush

You run, or start to, taking on the night again.
Muggers can't harm you when you have earphones in
tuned to Rap FM, pressing buttons through your gloves,

then something classical. A phone-in.
You are running off doors slamming; being
crushed between voices like a fly between fingernails.

That plane could be a hurled star and the moon
is identifiably the same as that beamed back
from the jinxed shuttle where astronauts

pointed at favourite constellations. Perseus,
one woman's choice: a hero securing a bride
as reward for his trials. Those pitiful stars

'I won't stop until I've travelled from one life to another'

you think, walking the last bit, past the garage,
your own windows, whose light-boxes house curious experiments
of the earthly kind relating to fathers and sons

and then there are choices – turn the key in the door,
stretch your limbs in the hall, or run, earphones
back in, past negatives of trees and cars.

JUSTINA HART

Running

I'm learning a new language
made of mud, hill, grass, puddle.
My body writes it on the wind –
wick, hi-vis, pronate, shin;
one mile, five, eight, ten.

It's a language of one foot
in front of the other.
I won't stop until I've travelled
from one life to another.

KATIE GREENBROWN

Someone else's bum

This is where I run, it's near my house, the sky is flung wide here for a town – for a time.
The rows of trees are crowns of broccolis, some lungs for me, for mine. And I can run for hours at a time here. As long as I don't mind slowing down for dogs and teenage smartphone frowns and prams and jogging nans and dogs in prams sometimes. But I don't mind. And I will always share this space with you. Watch the balloons go up with you.

Once, twice around if I've got time. Another runner smiles we pass again, our faces just the same but redder. We feel we are in this together. Alone but better for the freedom it gives. Dispel last night's drunk-too-much-guilt or can't rid my head of how it felt. Spill the beans to the air, no hurt caused there. Yes, this is a place I love and I will always smile and share this space with you.

But now the course is lined with mini buses. Three, four parked right across my path. Touching nearly, nose to tail, with rusting paint – not well-maintained. And each side door slides. Deposits fifteen men apiece on to the tarmac. They crouch or stand and smoke. Unsure, unmanned, un-warmly clothed. A plastic bag clutched in each hand. They're not local. Never here before. I guess this from the way they stand and look around and stretch their sore, too-long-bus-journey legs. And from the way they are took up and put down in this strange manner. A handful of tracksuits and anything shoes. Tipped on the turf. Zips un-catched. No two shoes a-match. Have they come to work like that?! No shave, no lunch, no anorak? Yes, now they begin to dismantle track.

And I watch and I'm afraid of what they'll say if I try to run past them dressed this way. And I need to run past them, but I want to stop and go the other way because I know what they'll say. They won't see that these leggings are tight to keep the sweat from my skin, or that figure-hugging tops are comfortable for running in. Or that she only ran out to put a flag on his horse, or what it feels like to choke when you're fed by force.

But going back is twice as far and it would make me a coward. And I need to get past and go home for a shower. And I will always smile and share this space with you. But now I am afraid of what they'll do. And I shouldn't be afraid and I shouldn't allow it, because they fought so we'd believe that we have a value. So it's okay for us to go and run alone. To dress how we want, no chaperone. So we're as good as our brothers, we're as clever as our brothers, we're as worthy of respect as others. And of course they're worthy of respect in turn because only an idiot believes that all men are pervs. So it won't happen really, because it would be the worst kind of cliché. But my heart beats faster because I know what they'll say. And I know what's going to happen and I know I'm getting nearer and I'm wishing now that lycra wasn't half so revealing.

Then I'm there. And it's awful. It's worse than I thought it would be. I want to cry but that's too easy so I close my eyes and I pick my speed up. But I'm humiliated and scared and I know that they're still there. And no one's going to tell them that it's not okay. And I'm not going to tell them that it's not okay. To shout and stare and gesture at another person in this way.

And you might say, oh just ignore it. It's just misguided banter. It's just what stupid lads do, especially in some cultures. And if you're so emancipated you should just shrug it off. And that you're lucky and you've read enough to understand the mixed-up, messed-up reasons for this stuff. But there were forty-five of them, and one of me. And no one seemed to realise that running clothes are tight for functionality. Not for titillation. Pardon the pun. Or so you get a really decent look at someone else's bum.

And they might be running too and they might need understanding, but I'd never undermine them or undress them with my eyes. And there's millennia of repression in what has just transpired. And who would ever let their children treat another human being in this way.

But I'll still go running because I love this place. And it's my tiny piece of bravery to smile and share this space with you. Even if you act like a bully or misogynist or bigot. Because I don't believe in labels, or that there's no good at all in you.

KERRY DARBISHIRE

Flight

When I think of running
I think of the foaming river
I had to cross to escape
the dark shape of him
shrugged   lurking
a panther   ready
at the end of the lane
his breath   a rope
hanging in damp air
                        I'm running
out of options   fast
winged   scared
jagged rocks biting
the thin soles of my sandals
along Wren's lane
fingery trees stroking
the turkey shed roof
up to the force
and back   slipping
through thickets of blackthorn   running
out of time   hope
heart pounding
like a grandfather clock
a deer   a fox   a hare
hounded to cover   den   lair
a child to home   running
through the village   away
from a November night

CAROLE BROMLEY

Twelve Reasons Why Not

Dogs
Lorry drivers whistling
Neighbours making remarks
Rain
Self-consciousness
Your belly
Making the time
Your laughable progress
Stage fright
Hitting the wall
The last half mile
Being overtaken by the pantomime camel

IAIN TWIDDY

Thawing River

This thaw, a lit Saturday afternoon,
running the blinky, blank-puddled track,
a gritty wind pitching at the boughs,

running with the bank-thrashing river,
the skewy crows and the full-throttle falls,
feebly, for the first time in weeks, it's clear

that the blocks of time in which I have lived
like snow stamped down into ice, are stacking up;
that it has to be here, at thirty-seven, or never,

that I begin to live like the river,
with the depth and surge of a thing itself,
a phenomenon only known in motion –

'I won't stop until I've travelled from one life to another'   121

yeah, begin to live like the thawing river,
irrespective of the distance left ahead,
unruffled by how much I have to catch up.

OLGA DERMOTT-BOND

M25, turning

A white horse on hard shoulder, galloping hard beside fields of traffic, fluency
of sweat in his flanks, sun's zoetrope, flickering through winter trees thin as
paper. Inside the ink-spill of its shadow I am turned a curious girl; my car
suddenly an attic in an old house, staring at this creature through a spinning
daedalum, thinking I must be the one making him run, veined and sinewed,
like this, like this, like this.

STEPHEN LIGHTBOWN

Running Together in Greenwich Park

I bring us here to run away.

Twenty years of sitting in the wheelchair
has left you fused like a sprinter
crouched on the starting line
legs bent, eager for the gun.

Pull running tights over fatless thighs.
Slide a vest over circus strongman chest,
tie laces. Limber, stretch.
Are you ready

to be lifted from day wheelchair
to racing wheelchair

four wheels to three, to fold
into position?

We share the same skin.
Wheelchair user. Runner.
Is this a single experience?

The early morning is empty. Like the chasm
that follows the words *you'll never walk again.*
I draw autumnal mist, back
beyond bare branches.

I stop pushing, see if you will take up the effort.
We drift, almost to a standstill.

Something approaching sadness
applies a brake.
It takes strength not made in a gym
to release it.

We pass the empty bandstand.
There's the sound of brass.
They came to play for us. Do you hear it?
This is where we won the city.

If you ask me
Is it still running
if our legs don't move?
I will say yes, though
I can't be sure you're listening.

STUART BARNES
Running In The Family

Cicadas unlashed their thunderous Morse
code. He and I zigzagged over a plover
-patrolled brown paddock, the uniform force

that'd scarred the old man dashing towards divorce
shooting through skies without cloud cover.
The indefatigable gorse

also enfolded fuzzy buds. Coarse
sounds crashed as we, two undercover
Doyles, tripped our grandfather's remorse

-less snares. It seemed to endorse
this crucial clash, the rusty barbed lover
of shins tuned out to the golf course.

A blue budgerigar with a hoarse
voice announced 'Winner!' To recover,
I splashed cold water; he hit the sauce.

Now he's inaccessible as Old Norse,
my poisonous cousin. What did he discover
on that boom-thrashed childhood concourse?
It's dragging him farther out, Wild Horse.

Note: Simon Doyle is a former Australian middle distance runner

VICTORIA GATEHOUSE
Snails

Those streets I ran with my dad
the weeks leading up to my divorce
were the streets of my childhood –
the huge oak on the corner where I'd turn
right for school, the ginnels I'd shoot
on my Raleigh, clipping privet, a scatter
of gravel in my wake. Aged thirty, a return
to the room I left at eighteen, my dad
saying nothing except *come for a run*
and I let him set the pace, so much slower
than I remembered, but steady
through the shortening evenings,
street-lit runnels of rain, gleaming
on root-lifted tarmac. Once or twice
he'd put a hand to my back as we kept
our eyes on the darkening ground,
tried to keep from crushing the snails.

MANDY SUTTER
Old Trail Runner

In winter, my father sets up base camp
in the one-man kitchen of his first floor flat,
hunkering by the radio, barely moving,
warmed by Calor gas and the thought
of cupboards crammed with canned
corned beef. Everything's to hand:
kettle, screwdriver, five pairs of specs.

At night, with stubborn care, he makes
the hard ascent, following the chimney up.

'I won't stop until I've travelled from one life to another'   125

The view is stunning. To spite the doctor
he forgets his tablets and, fortified
by sherry and bananas, wearing a woolly hat,
bivvies on the bed-ledge; wakes
to ice on the inside of the window.

He believes in north and south, in pass
or fail. He doesn't want a Sherpa,
has no fear of heights or falling boulders;
looks up to the wolf moon. He's acclimatizing
for his next summit, the one he'll run
solo, following his long-lost brother's
route to the ridge, and on, and up.

DI SLANEY
Bildr's thorp

He ran from the farm like he was learning to slay,
great grandfather's hounds snouting his heels
with low battle howls, an invisible axe twirling
through grass downhill to the ditch. The half-
remembered hearthtale of severed hands
hovered somewhere north, somewhere hard
and cold and red, somewhere near a shore
far from here, when boats were more
important than carts and jewels as big as
skimstones pinned the eyelids of the dead.
Nothing was owned or held, only wanted.
Movement was everything and settlement a
rumour of old age few would see, or wish for.
He ran from the softness of straw and the comfort
of cattle. He ran because his mother called him
darling, kept him closer than the hounds and
tighter than the bindings on his fox fur boots.
And as he ran, something small and fierce burned

'I won't stop until I've travelled from one life to another'

through his chest until it burst on his tongue,
sprayed through the story of the morning in
one long eulalia, herald warrior in waiting
for a past buried under this rocky mound, safe
behind the ramparts of his father's steading.

KATHARINE GODA

Running Away

They said
my heart beat
too slowly

I had to eat
to feed it

my children
needed me.

This heart
which beat
three lives
into being

powered
fell runs
stream leaps
new PBs

grieved
silent and
unsteady

still beats,
slowly.

ESTELLE PRICE

Running after dark in Homa Bay County

Night drops like a black stone
into the compound. A dusty shirt, static
in a plastic bucket, turns water to rust;
chickens huddle in a tin shed; a kerosene lamp
is lit. Swaddled, his wife and son dream away
the day's thunder, not knowing they'll be
alone for hours, not knowing this man's

a night runner. Naked, acacia stick in fist,
he abandons the mud-walled hut to swing
through the bush. What will he be tonight?
A gorilla, a dog, a cobra? He's faster
than an Olympic sprinter, his warlock tongue's
on fire. With one finger he can paralyse
an eagle, with one slap he can seal a man's

ears. Like a bearded vulture he hijacks a roof,
casts spells down the chimney until fear
knots a neighbour's hair. When sun displaces
moon, he skips to bed. At worship he'll kneel
in the white church on the hill, recite prayers
his mama taught him, remember how his baba
bid him answer God's call to run through the black.

JON MCLEOD

Blake on his morning run sees angels in a tree

As a child he was whipped for it,
now it's part of his Sunday routine,
the long run past the workhouse,
the whorehouse, the demonic windmills

out onto terrain more suitable for visions.
They see him first, their silver hair catching
the breeze in the birches. They beckon
with their lightly-sketched hands,
mouths barely opening for solicitations.

For them, time is a supreme irrelevance,
but they feign interest in his personal
best for the Echoing Green
to the Garden of Love. They are pleased
he is doing London this year
as it needs a complete makeover,
and if he can chase away
some ironmasters, that would be
a big help on the whole.

He returns in higher spirits
to sit naked in the garden
with Mrs B, who admires
his ample thigh muscles
and reminds him that the tiger
in the outhouse requires a second coat.

RISHI DASTIDAR

Unhalting

for Alan Turing

So many hypotheses he cracked & cracked,
an enigma that blew BOMBEs, hastened
an end, brought forward the future;
and yet there was one thing that wouldn't
yield to his logic, patterned on long runs
from Bletchley to London – what is it to be
human; or rather, how do you compute it,
how do you prove it? This was his decision

problem, and while he knew the body was
connected to the spirit, the algorithm
suggested the spirit would never stop.

GILES GOODLAND

Sewage

Passing under the lime tree
a certain angle of early sunlight
catches the aphid-frass, or perhaps
pollen (it is spring) falling, finer
than rain, more gold. Seen between alleys,
the river oxbows through fly-
dumped meadows, is culverted
under the slip road, then a long
duck-boarded sequence (Saturday and
I meet no one) coarsens gradually
through a golf-course where the pollen-filmed
ditch widens into a dandelion-fluff-
strewn channel down to a railway, grubby
reflections of multilingual
bright graffiti, sifting it, head down,
the tunnel comes out on the heath,
still-smoking mopeds, furze, bramblings, stream-noise
a large iron gate I can push open, onto
warehouses, post office depots, another
high street, alleys, then reedbeds,
stench. Pipes strut towards a concrete tower.
Here pause long enough to sense
the wind through sedge, three
blackbirds fighting, an alder, puddles,
a wartime pillbox. The hum and seethe.
One bird turns its head rapidly.
Last week's rain comes out as leaves.
A satellite view would show the circles,

suggest by coloration the sludge
settling, but I get the ammoniac
knock at my olfactory gates.
Scrub this, purify, settle the loss. Weeks
pass through the system until the river
comes clean. Matter is parted. Spirit
settles: our sediments are sunk in thought.

JULIE MACLEAN

Thread Lines

after Carlo Giambarresi

When the moment feels right
a woman must take

a supersized ball of yarn
Pin the loose end

to that place
just above the heart

Put on a pair of breathing
socks and cast off

She will find herself
in strange and familiar

lands   wearing her first
love as a vest   others

as a warm scarf
the child her life's work

There will be times
scrambling over

mountain spines –
The Pennines and Pyrenees

The Great Dividing Range
she will stop   just stop

for whatever reason
She will drop stitches

and wear the air
Sometimes her skin will crack

LORRAINE MARINER

Running, Like an Old Flame

At the age when athletes retire, running called
on me again. Said *It's been over twenty years
but it's not too late*. It led me to Greenwich Park
and told me I had just as much right to be there
as the lovers and the kids on wheels and the dogs.
It dressed me in quick-drying, breathable spandex,
the most expensive shoes I have ever bought,
and made me download disco beats on to an iPod.
My legs and my lungs remembered what to do.
I got regular doses of daylight, and the seasons
framed and changing by increments. I got faster.
I swear some of the dogs, whose owners could only
walk, wished they belonged to me. And I prayed *Knees,
oh my forty-year-old knees, don't take this away from me.*

HELEN ALLISON

Culbin Forest 5K

for Julie Lawson

Our faces cold water splashed and just out of bed,
I am luminous yellow, you are fleece-lined in purple.
The birch trees stretch loose-limbed into morning,
our breathy chat startling the birds, but leaving
the pond ice intact, our rise and descent gravelled
and pine-scented, the shifting sands solid under our feet.
We waste nothing here, not word or minute, the path
to the sea always ahead, a dip saved for the next life.

SARAH VENART

I Believe You Still Have My Key

He doesn't live inside me I think as I run past cigarette can,
deadwood bench, the man with his too-large tongue hanging out.

A halfway house should be called a waiting house, you once said.
No two ways about it.

I am not proud of how I treated you, passing by
your cloud of need, doing nothing with my thoughts

but thinking. Could be better,
could be sweet. Somewhere around nineteen, doubt closed me

like a dress seam.
Inside were sealed all your reminders

not to live too much in my ideas,
to live instead

in your plans. I bit myself around the nails
to try to let you out.

Now I'm like those fields I've seen recuperating in clover
after years of potatoes.

At the corner of our street the man with the tongue
hangs out in his waiting house. No matter where I run

ideas get taken down by doubt. Give me back
my key. I feel you take it

like a verb from your pants pocket
to scrape along my thigh.

LUCY HOLT

once you're on you can't get off

you'd think tiring yourself out would
tire you out more
but no
here we are
once you start it's hard to stop
counting sheep on the elliptical
Countryfile's on with the sound turned down
or maybe there no sound to begin with

later the clagginess of dream-running
contains its own instructions
I flail spectacularly with my wednesday limbs (a joke)
the punchline being: whens they going to snap?
I used to be offended by that

the bulb blows the car lurches forward
TV Bad Boy Richard Hillman Drives
The Platts Into A Canal (2003)

we topple over all the different edges
at the edge of all the different edge dreams
over and over and over

I've left the big light on
not particularly imaginative in near-sleep
apparently now I have to
scoop up bits of confetti from the floor
and put them where
my stomach ought to go

after I've tidied up I wake jaw-first
into some much worser state
with a dithering chest
and a shiny forehead
and – you know –
that *licheny* taste

never before have I felt more awake
never again will I be this good at maths
Richard can we go again
baby you're a running machine
from the top
once more around the block

LYDIA ALLISON

Inevitable

I ran today with Amy Winehouse. What
a woman, what a voice, what a take
on shitty things in life.
                    She sheds some light
upon her own goodbyes, her beating heart
reluctant. I'm in love with her. She's my
best friend.

She talks to me as though she's not
alone, but I don't mind. My absent man:
a man we share; a secret that we split
in half and carry:
                    shoulders bony, bare.
She speaks as though there's things she can't avoid.
My legs catch every lurch I make, unthinking.
Amy's right.
                    It feels like fate. My run-through life.

ANNE RYLAND

Sunday, on the run

along the ramparts, under the gate and away
from fortifications and paternal timetables,
the toll of a bell slows me – if I were in a pew,
stilled, I might question my flights into dawn.
I'm running from the things I have left undone.
From the house and its press cupboards,
its brown blots; reminders we are not watertight.
I'm running from eye-wipes and artificial
teardrops and, even now, from the pelvic years.
I need to break loose from the anthology
of anxieties, from those notebooks too exquisite
for notes. Untroubled by speed, I'm running from
that vexing verb *relax*
                    towards the sea wall,
to go quiet, be distilled –
a yellow sign casts me as a woman proceeding
at her own risk; strangely hydrating.
I'm running for a dewy smirr on my arms.
I'm running because my thighs are able.
The earth is generous; I'm running towards a path
towards a threshold, where my feet will learn
cadence, and with soft strokes my body
will start writing its own footnotes.

'I won't stop until I've travelled from one life to another'

ERIN WILSON
Running as Birdsong

Having had the same legs. Having had the same body. Having had the same brain. Running through the same woods. Running up the same road. Running by way of the same machine. Turning over the same distance. Turning by cadence the same rocks. Turning beneath the same sphincter of sunlight. Thoughts changing.

Moving as though a part of the kaleidoscope. Moving linearly. Understanding then and now. Understanding then and now will move like the ladder rungs into the future. Nevertheless, sun spatter on the bones like light on the understory. Moving as part of the kaleidoscope. Separating. Dividing. Merging. Picking up on old patterns. Remembering by points, your convergence. Running forward and diverging. Understanding one can not possibly remember it all.

So. Forgetting It All.

But remembering some of it. Remembering some as though it's encoded in your body. Remembering some as though your will is mute. Remembering some as though you are inarticulate matter. Remembering by way of forgetfulness of the self. You are the swamp and its seasons without sentiment.

Then a sudden rush of sentiment returning. Remembering yourself distinct as you move through the distance. Distance which is, in its epitome, birdsong. Birdsong being eternal. Birdsong transcending the bird. You are one bird. And so much less than one too.

About the Authors

Mara Adamitz Scrupe is the author of four poetry collections: *Sky Pilot* (Finishing Line Press, 2012), *BEAST*, (Stevens Manuscript Prize, 2014), *Magnalia*, (Eyewear Press, 2018) and *A Daughter's Aubade/ Sailing Out from Sognefjord* (Middle Creek Press, 2018). She is the winner of the 2018 Grindstone Literary International Poetry Competition, and has been shortlisted for poetry awards including Wenlock Prize, Bridport Prize, Aesthetica Creative Writing Award and the National Poetry Society Competition. For over twenty-five years she has lived, and run, with rheumatoid arthritis; she has finished four marathons and won the 2015 Philadelphia Marathon in her class (3:44) at age sixty. She finds peace, meditation and strength running alone.

Josie Alford has an MA in Creative Writing from Bath Spa University. She hosts the Hammer and Tongue Slams in Bristol and is part of the team who won the slam at the National Finals in 2018. Her poems have been published in *Ink, Sweat and Tears* and *Obsessed With Pipework*.

Helen Allison is a slow runner and a lazy one without a friend, or the promise of trees. She runs in her home town of Forres, passing monuments and supermarkets, forgetting her father's motto of 'Don't get off the pavement for anyone.' Her favourite run is in a nearby forest on the Moray coast, its rich history and calm air make her forget to let her terrible sense of direction hold her back.

Lydia Allison is a poet from Sheffield. She tends to run in Rivelin Valley and finds it's a great time to be alone, to think, and to listen to music. She also enjoys running with friends and some of her poetry is influenced by the halted (but eventually successful) conversations they have on the way.

Abeer Ameer is originally from Iraq but was made in England like the blue Cortina. Her poems have appeared in *Acumen*, *Planet Magazine*, *The Interpreter's House*, *Tears in the Fence*, *Envoi*, *Prole*, *Barzakh Magazine*, *Atrium* and *LossLit Magazine*. She is currently working on a collection of poems based on personal stories from Iraq.

Jane Aspinall grew up in Liverpool and was a first stage winner in the 2009 /10 Poetry Business Competition. Andrew Motion described her work as 'managing to pull off the difficult trick of being at once valiant and vulnerable'. Her poem 'Tambourine' took second place at the Academi Cardiff International Poetry Competition in 2010 and since then Jane has run several half marathons, studied for an MA in Screenwriting and continues to read and write poetry.

Stuart Barnes, a runner waylaid by sciatica, was born in Hobart and raced around Melbourne for seventeen years before darting to Rockhampton. His first poetry collection, *Glasshouses* (UQP), won the Thomas Shapcott Prize and was shortlisted/commended for two other awards. Since 2017 Stuart's been a program advisor for Queensland Poetry Festival. He daydreams often about middle distance running and is currently working on his second poetry collection, *Form & Function*.

Alison Binney is an English teacher, poet and runner from Cambridge. The flat fenland landscape makes for easy, if not especially exciting, running, and her usual route is along the towpath beside the River Cam. She regularly competes in 10k races, enjoying the series of Hoohah events at nearby National Trust estates. She's also participated several times in the Cambridge Half Marathon. She finds that when she gets stuck with a poem, going for a run can often be helpful.

Julian Bishop is a London-based former journalist and poet who writes most of his work while running in the gym, using his phone's Notes feature to write and then refining them on a PC at home. He was recently runner-up in the international Ginkgo Eco-Poetry Prize.

David Borrott lives in Lancashire. His pamphlet *Porthole* was published by Smith|Doorstop as part of their Laureate's Choice Series. He was awarded a Northern Writers Award in 2015.

Rachel Bower lives in Sheffield with her three young children. She is also a poet and Leverhulme Research Fellow at the University of Leeds. Although all of this is wonderful, life is very busy and Rachel loves the freedom of running and temporarily leaving all of the different aspects of her life behind. This is sometimes about re-remembering who she is, even a question of survival of the self. She loves running in all seasons; in the Peaks and down Sheffield's streets.

Carole Bromley lives in York which is flat and ideal for running. At school she was a sprinter rather than a distance runner. She did once train for a 5k despite self-consciousness, fear of dogs and sexist remarks. That was thirty years ago and she still has the medal! These days she's more likely to run on a treadmill or go for a brisk walk but she's never forgotten the buzz which running gave her.

Michael Brown began running in 2001 to lose weight. He set his 10k PB in 2001 in his first ever 'proper race' (Leeds Abbey Dash). It still stands (43.02). Since then he has completed 450+ parkruns, one marathon and several half-marathons. He is a slow starter and a strong finisher, often passing push-chairs and runners in fancy dress in the sprint for the line.

Alan Buckley is from Merseyside, and now lives in Oxford. Despite never having been a runner himself he still felt entitled to talk about the psychology of running to a friend who was. 'Run' is his poetic apology to her. His most recent publication is *The Long Haul* (HappenStance, 2016). He is a poetry editor at ignitionpress, and a school writer-in-residence with First Story.

Lewis Buxton is a poet, performer, arts producer and runner. His work has appeared in *Ambit*, *Magma* & *Oxford Poetry* and won the Poetry School & Nine Arches Press Primers competition. He grew up in North London where he ran up its many hills. He now lives in Norwich where there are very few hills.

Joe Caldwell is a poet and teacher from Sheffield. His writing has been published in various magazines and anthologies. He enjoys a variety of sports, including running, but the serious runner in the household is his wife, Siân, who gets round a marathon in around three hours.

Niall Campbell was born in Scotland and lives in Leeds. He received an Eric Gregory Award in 2011, an Arvon-Jerwood Mentorship in 2013, and won the Poetry London Competition in 2013. His first book-length collection, *Moontide* (Bloodaxe Books, 2014), won the Edwin Morgan Poetry Award, the Saltire First Book of the Year Award, was shortlisted for the Forward Prize for Best First Collection, the Fenton Aldeburgh First Collection Prize and the Michael Murphy Memorial Prize, and is a Poetry Book Society Recommendation.

Mark Carson has a contrarian view of running. He thinks this view should be included in the anthology to give balance to the collection, which otherwise may be overloaded with sweaty enthusiasm. His favourite run is the Cresta.

Duncan Chambers detested sport at school but started running for exercise in his forties and was surprised to find that he enjoyed it. He has completed about 20 marathons (including one in the Swiss Alps) but most enjoys cross-country (especially afterwards) and the inclusiveness of his local parkrun in York.

Eric Chandler is the author of *Hugging This Rock: Poems of Earth & Sky, Love & War* (Middle West Press, 2017). He's a husband, father, and pilot who lives in Duluth, Minnesota. Chandler uses cross-country skiing as an excuse for why his Grandma's Marathon is so slow each year. Then, annually, he blames running for his slow American Birkebeiner ski marathon. He prefers trails to roads, but he's grateful he can run anywhere at all.

Oliver Comins has fond memories of cross country races through ploughed fields, wet woods and across cold hills. Nowadays, he charges round with a little more decorum and a lot less mud. His first full-length collection of poems, *Oak Fish Island*, was published by Templar Poetry in 2018.

Noel Connor ran everywhere as a child, seeing little point in walking. Qualifying for the Belfast School Sports, he was shocked and disheartened on the start line, to realise he was the only child still wearing clumpy school shoes and not trainers. He didn't win. Now primarily a visual artist, he exhibits widely in Ireland and Britain, but remains most proud of an early school report describing him as 'a great wee half miler'.

Mark Connors is a poet and novelist from Leeds. He began running on New Year's Day 2014 on the Couch to 5k programme and has been running regularly ever since. He began running to help himself stop smoking and is now training for his second 50 mile Ultra Marathon. He aims to run a 100k in one day before his 50th birthday next year.

Suzanne Conway Suzanne Conway came close to running 800m for Great Britain. It is still a sadness to her it didn't happen. Solace comes in running the country lanes, woods and hills. She has published twenty-five poems in magazines and anthologies, including *The Poetry Review*, *The North* and *The Moth*. She is working towards her first collection.

Anthony Costello runs on the moors, on a transcendental journey. The physical, mental and emotional states feel out of time, but he's in a place he wants to be. Running is about the present, but running's transitory nature is realised with every step, so the runner wants to run again. Injuries are obstacles, so runners, aware their bodies are in a state of increasing mortal ruin, make 'running pacts' with the Faust in themselves.

Geoff Cox is a Lake District based fellrunner and, in his 64th year, old enough to know better. He loves long, lonely days out in the fells though these days often turn, inexplicably, into long nights. He doesn't like crowds, so rarely races, and has recently developed a habit of writing old-fashioned poetry about his runs. He has discovered that this is an even better way of avoiding crowds.

Kerry Darbishire is a songwriter/poet and lives in Cumbria. Her poems appear widely in anthologies and magazines and have won competition prizes including being shortlisted for the Bridport Prize 2017. Her first poetry collection, *A Lift of Wings*, was published in 2014 by Indigo Dreams and a biography, *Kay's Ark*, was published in 2016 by Handstand Press. Her second poetry collection, *Distance Sweet on my Tongue*, (Indigo Dreams Press, 2018) was a finalist in the Cumbria Culture Awards 2019. Kerry can't run but admires those who can.

Rishi Dastidar's poetry has been published by the Financial Times and the BBC amongst many others. His collection *Ticker-tape* is published by Nine Arches Press; a poem from it was included in The Forward Book of Poetry 2018. Having completed four half marathons, he retains a fading hope that he might break 1h 30m in a future race; right now he's focusing on trying to reach the black level in the Nike Run Club app.

Olga Dermott-Bond's way of running is to start slowly and get slower. She dislikes running up hills but has to, as someone put lots of them around her house. Headspace, health and creativity are the reasons that she runs. Olga has had poetry and flash-fiction published in a range of magazines and was one of the winners of the 2018 BBC Proms poetry competition. She is a teacher and has two daughters.

Mike Di Placido found running was a major part of his life into his mid-twenties. As a footballer it was an obvious requirement, although he never strayed far from the opposition penalty area! He loved distance running too, and thinks there's a correlation between running and the creative process. He's sure it aligns with Ted Hughes's description of his mental state when watching his float while fishing, as: 'entering one of the orders of bliss'.

Pat Edwards found running was always a kind of therapy. She's very jealous seeing fellow sixty-somethings who can still do it. Although she occasionally breaks into a mild trot, she's left behind proper wind-in-your-hair running for curating a poetry festival. As an ex-PE teacher she still promotes jogging as exercise you can do on your own without expensive equipment; the best way to feel utterly alive.

Nell Farrell loves running but is sometimes thwarted by the after-effects of a slipped disc long ago. She tries not to run on concrete, so woods, fields, allotment paths and beaches are her favourite territories.

Mike Farren is a poet, publisher and all-too occasional runner. His pamphlet, *Pierrot and his Mother*, was published by Templar in 2017, two years after he completed his only half marathon, The Great North Run (in which he failed to trouble Mo Farah). With a handful of 10k's to his name, he fancies being an octogenarian marathon runner but doesn't want to wear himself out before then. His second pamphlet, *All of the Moons*, is published by Yaffle.

Mark Fiddes covers 10k slowly anywhere he can find a route. His favorite trail is the Carros de Foc, a high mountain run in the Pyrenees, although he also likes cities on race days. He is published by Templar Poetry (*The Chelsea Flower Show Massacre* and *The Rainbow Factory*). Other work has appeared recently in *The Irish Times*, *Magma*, *Poem International*, *The London Magazine* and *Aesthetica*.

Julia Forster started running at the age of 22 when she realised that running was just walking, but faster. She was introduced to it while living with two women in Brooklyn who would run up and down the stairwells of skyscrapers in Manhattan for fun. Now 40, Julia runs up and down the hills surrounding Machynlleth with friends on an irregular basis, and loves the opportunity to chat just as much as the exercise.

Victoria Gatehouse is a West Yorkshire based poet and was one of the few who actually enjoyed cross country running at school. She held the school record for 800m and ran competitively in her youth. Now she runs far more slowly and less often, sometimes with friends and occasionally still with her dad. Walking has overtaken running and most days she is out striding the Pennines with her dog, Obi Wan Kenobi.

Katharine Goda started writing poems and running at about the same time. Both give her space to notice tiny details of extraordinary-everyday life and to work out what she's thinking and feeling. Ideally early, air crisp, imagining she's the first up, when people still smile conspiratorially. Somewhere wind-blown and full of its own noises – beach, hills, moors. Home to a hot shower, warm drink, the rest of the house still asleep.

John Goodby was born in Birmingham, and now lives in Wales and Yorkshire; his first poetry collection was *A Birmingham Yank* (Arc, 1988). He began to run, along the shining curve of Swansea Bay, about ten years ago. He enjoys the fruitful paradox of running; that, while it subordinates the self to the body, its insistent rhythms can take the runner beyond the physical realm to the point where running becomes a form of meditation.

Giles Goodland started running 'seriously' about 10 years ago, at the age of 45, when he was about three stone overweight and developing musculoskeletal problems. It was his aim to run a marathon before the age of 50, and after a couple of failures he succeeded. Now in his mid-50s runs are more obser-vational, stopping to take notes and observe. Resident in West London and disliking pavements, his runs are often attempts to draw together green spaces: canal paths, tracks, parks. His books are published by Salt and Shearsman.

Mark Granier's fifth collection, *Ghostlight: New & Selected Poems*, was pub-lished by Salmon in 2017. He started jogging in his late twenties and kept it up till recently, after he turned 60. Thinking about this theme, he remembered his first, abbreviated jog, and his mother's surprised laughter at how quickly he reappeared, utterly shagged. Also an odd dream: running his favourite route, a forest track, carrying a small bag of belongings (wallet, shoes, etc.) looking for somewhere to stow it. But more and more people kept turning up, and the bag grew to a huge, awkward box he had to somehow hold together as he kept running.

Katie Greenbrown is a writer and performer of Spoken Word with links to York's Say Owt and the North's spoken word scene. She won Say Owt Slam in 2017 and was awarded York Culture Award's Best Performing Artist. When she's not writing and performing, she runs. Favourite routes include the shady pathways along the Ouse and racecourse. She runs to clear her mind and form new ideas, and uses the time to memorise her work.

Nicky Hallett runs each day come rain or shine in one of Sheffield's many parks. It is a lifeline. She ran as a child, then stopped for over forty years, so is now slow, not really very sure, but extremely determined. If you read Vybarr Cregan-Reid, *Footnotes: How Running Makes Us Human*, you'll understand kinetic empathy: She tries to.

Charles Hamilton Sorley was born in Scotland in 1895. He enlisted in the British Army and was sent to the Western Front as a lieutenant in the Suffolk Regiment. Sorley was killed by a sniper at the Battle of Loos on October 13th 1915. Thirty-seven of his poems were published posthumously as *Marlborough and Other Poems* (Cambridge University Press, 1916).

Stuart Handysides took to cross-country running at school in Derbyshire and Newcastle-under-Lyme, and came back to it later to clear his head in the middle of the working day, digest the stressy soup in his circulation, satisfy the twitchy muscles. His poems have appeared in *London Grip New Poetry*, *The North*, *Pennine Platform*, *Presence*, and *South* magazines. He has run (yes, pun) the Ware Poets competition for several years.

Justina Hart lives and writes aboard a historic narrowboat moored in Staffordshire. Her pamphlet *Remapping* was shortlisted in the Poetry School's 2014 competition. She was commissioned by Durham University and Free Word and TippingPoint in 2016 to write a long climate change poem, and received an Artists' International Development Fund Award in 2018 to perform it in Australia. She started running after a relationship break-up and loves cross-country. She now runs on the towpath.

Tracey Herd was born in Scotland in 1968 and lives in Edinburgh. She studied at Dundee University, where she was Creative Writing Fellow in 1998-2001. In 1993 she won an Eric Gregory Award, and in 1995 a Scottish Arts Council Bursary. She has published three collections, *No Hiding Place* (1996), which was shortlisted for the Forward Prize for Best First Collection; *Dead Redhead* (2001), a Poetry Book Society Recommendation; and *Not in This World* (2015), a Poetry Book Society Choice shortlisted for the T S Eliot Prize, all with Bloodaxe.

Jan Heritage was talked into training for the London Marathon twenty years ago and hasn't stopped running since. While she likes the thrill of crossing a finishing line, she also runs to explore an unfamiliar city or a new landscape; to resolve a problem, write a poem, meet a friend or deal with a loss. On Saturday mornings you'll find her on Brighton seafront supporting the local parkrun: the brilliant, volunteer-led, free 5k that's encouraging many to start running. Favourite runs: early morning solitary on the South Downs and/or the magnificent cheering crowds of London. an is the editor of *Finished Creatures* poetry magazine.

Geoffrey Hill was born in Worcestershire, England in 1932. He was the author of seven books of poems: *For the Unfallen* (1959), *King Log* (1968), *Mercian Hymns* (1971), *Tenebrae* (1978), *The Mystery of the Charity of Charles Peguy* (1983), *Canaan* (1997), and *The Triumph of Love* (1998). He received awards including the Hawthornden and Whitbread Prizes, as well as the Loines Award and a special citation for poetry from the American Academy and Institute of Arts and Letters. Hill died in 2016. Posthumous works published include *The Book of Baruch by the Gnostic Justin* (2019).

Lizzie Holden is a London poet. Her poems are primarily about love and loss. Themes of abuse, dance, trees and breath also find their way into poem-shaped forms. Her poems have been published by *Sable Books*, *The Emma Press*, *Picaroon Poetry*, *Medusa's Laugh Press*, *Dream Catcher*, *Live Canon*, *Kind of a Hurricane Press* and *The Frogmore Papers*. 'The Ten Percent' was commended in the Glebe House International Poetry Competition and 'Routine' was longlisted in the Live Canon 2018 International Poetry competition.

Lucy Holt is a writer from Manchester. She studied at the University of Sheffield where it's impossible to run because of the hills. She later worked as a copywriter, and is now doing an MA in Writing at The Royal College of Art, London. She is terrible at running but is fascinated by it, especially in relation to bodies, rituals, dreams, weird online wellness culture and what Rebecca Solnit calls the 'aerobic sisyphus' of the gym.

Alfred Edward Housman was born in Worcestershire in 1859, the eldest of seven children. Housman published two volumes of poetry during his life: *A Shropshire Lad* (1896) and *Last Poems* (1922). A third volume, *More Poems*, was released posthumously in 1936 by his brother, Laurence, as was an edition of *Housman's Complete Poems* (1939). He died on April 30, 1936, in Cambridge.

Jack Houston and his partner spend their time 'running' a household which includes two under-fives – a marathon in itself! Elsewhere, he staffs for Hackney's public libraries and his partner is a counsellor. His work has appeared in *And Other Poems, Brittle Star, The Butcher's Dog, Interpreter's House, Magma* and a few others, and has also been shortlisted for the Keats-Shelley, the Basil Bunting Prizes and has taken 2nd place in the 2017 Poetry London Competition.

Paul Howarth is a writer, a photographer and a librarian. He lives near the Suffolk coast with his wife and two boys. Paul has taken part in various 10k events and half-marathons, most recently he completed the Great East Run. He is currently trying to get his head around the logical next step – a full marathon. However, he runs mostly to find space, to connect with his landscape and because he knows it's good for him.

Rae Howells is a poet and journalist from Swansea. She is an inconsistent runner with dodgy hips and two daughters. Fitness, being outdoors and getting to her destination on time are her main motivations for running. Her poems have appeared in the *Rialto, Magma, New Welsh Review, Envoi, Marble* and *Poetry Ireland* and she has won both the Rialto and International Welsh poetry competitions.

Cynthia X Hua is a poet and artist. She was previously a Finalist for the Norman Mailer Awards in Poetry, and nominated for a Pushcart Prize. She grew up running through deserts and valleys in California.

Vicki Husband's first collection of poetry, *This Far Back Everything Shimmers*, was shortlisted for The Saltire Society Poetry Book of the Year 2016. Vicki was an Edinburgh Southern Harrier in her youth; she rediscovered running in her late 30's. After work Vicki can often be found running around Pollok Park in Glasgow; favourite routes include the trails & hills of the West Highland Way, the Pentlands and the Arrochar Alps.

Jenny King's experience of running started in childhood – dashing to the pillar box with a letter and arriving back in less than two minutes to astonish her mother – and never got much further. She's intrigued and impressed, however, by the determination of people going for a run along the street or streaming past the bus in great numbers on a Saturday parkrun.

Igor Klikovac is a Bosnian poet living in London since 1993. His work is published in Bosnia, countries of former Yugoslavia, Britain, and elsewhere. *Stockholm Syndrome* was published by Smith|Doorstop in 2018.

Liz Lefroy's untreated asthma took the fun out of school cross-country. Now, equipped with an inhaler, she is a fan of the parkrun movement and its inclusivity. Running in Krakow, and reaching her 50th parkrun in 2018 at her local Shrewsbury course are running highlights. Poetry highlights have included winning the 2011 Roy Fisher prize and the 2016 Café Writers Prize, and reading on Carol Ann Duffy's 2016 Shore to Shore tour.

Stephen Lightbown is Blackburn born and Bristol based. Stephen is paralysed from below the waist following an accident when he was 16. He writes poetry extensively, but not exclusively, about his life as a wheelchair user. Stephen uses his arms to run and has completed marathons in London and Berlin and more than a dozen half marathons and 10ks. He has shared a lift with Jessica Ennis-Hill and given Roger Black directions to a running track.

Julie Lumsden was very nippy as a child, darting everywhere. She remembers enjoying racing up stairs, especially in the house where she had an attic bedroom. Some people reach a stage where they may take part in a parents' race at school sports day (She did this once and fell over). She never runs now, just walks very quickly for buses she thinks she might miss.

Julie Maclean ponders Haruki Murakami before she thinks of running – 'Pain is inevitable. Suffering is optional'. She runs around the house and once dashed through Palm Valley in outback Australia using smooth rocks as stepping stones. She is the author of five racy poetry collections and is widely published and anthologised in international journals.

Lorraine Mariner lives where Blackheath meets Greenwich Park, the London Marathon start, and watching the runners set off inspired her to take up running after not running since school. Her favourite place to run is on the heath (on the grass alongside the paths to protect her knees), finishing up in the park. She has run half-marathons and hopes to run the London Marathon one day but hasn't been lucky in the ballot so far.

Alwyn Marriage has for years enjoyed the occasional morning run, frequently arriving back with a new poem in tow. She decided this year to take up the challenge of Couch to 5k, either on the nearby downs or through local woods, and by the ninth week was running for thirty minutes three times a week without too much difficulty. She now manages to run 5k twice a week, and enjoys her local parkrun.

Jonathan Mayman's parents' old photo album includes a black and white Kodak print of him aged two, on the lawn in their garden with the caption *Jonny running* and next to it another captioned *Jonny … still running*. At school he competed in everything – sprints, middle distance, cross-country. In later life he was lucky enough to keep up road-running into his sixties till grounded by a heart blip. He misses it.

Beth McDonough attempted a Parkrun in 2017, and surprised herself. Since, she's run a 10-mile race and is preparing for her first half marathon. To cool down, she swims year-round in the Tay. Both madnesses bring poems and peace. She is published in various places including *Gutter*, *Agenda* and *Poetry Salzburg Review*. She reviews with DURA, and co-wrote *Handfast* with Ruth Aylett. She's now running towards her first solo pamphlet in 2019.

Nicholas McGaughey is part of the Literature Wales Mentoring Initiative 2019. He is an ex-marathon runner who hung up his shoes after twenty good years running up and down the hillsides of The Rhondda. He ran with his father for many years, for charity and the hell of it usually awarding themselves copious pints afterwards. He used to run to work and back along The Taff Trail to save money and stay fit.

Laura McKee wanted to try running to boost serotonin levels as a back up for antidepressants when nearing her 55th birthday. Expecting to be discouraged, she googled whether it would be safe for a large asthmatic lady with family history of osteoporosis and instead found real life success stories, so then had no excuse. Randomly, while out walking, she ran up the steps and over a motorway bridge. She was breathless but glowing, laughing, and immediately hooked.

Jon McLeod was born in South Australia, grew up in West Cumbria and now lives near Blackpool. He took up running just under twenty years ago and has achieved remarkable mediocrity at a wide range of distances including the full marathon. Despite personal bests being well behind him, he's determined to plod on and think of the odd poem along the way.

Rachael Mead is a South Australian poet, writer, arts critic and very slow runner. Her previous books of poetry include *The Sixth Creek* (Picaro, 2013) and *The Flaw in the Pattern* (UWAP, 2018). Her regular long runs are either through the Adelaide Hills or beside the sea but, as a frequent traveller, her

150

favourite way to explore a new place is an early morning run along its riverside running path.

Julie Mellor holds a PhD from Sheffield Hallam University. Her pamphlets, *Breathing Through Our Bones* (2012) and *Out of the Weather* (2017), are published by Smith|Doorstop. Having always lagged behind on the school cross country, she continues to keep an eye out for a convenient field to cut across and dreams of sprinting to the finish without being caked in mud.

Helen Mort is a five-times winner of the Foyle Young Poets of the Year Competition, and her work has been shortlisted for the Costa Prize and the T S Eliot Prize. She is a Fellow of the Royal Society of Literature. Her poetry collections *Division Street* and *No Map Could Show Them* are published by Chatto & Windus. She is a Lecturer in Creative Writing at Manchester Metropolitan University. She has edited an anthology of poems for children, *The Owl and the Pussycat*. In 2017, she worked with Stuart Maconie to edit *One For The Road: An Anthology of Pubs and Poetry* (Smith|Doorstop, 2017). She has also edited *Waymaking*, a book of adventure-inspired art and literature by women.

Diane Mulholland was born in rural Australia and now lives in London. She hasn't lost her love of the outdoors, and takes every chance to explore what wilderness she can find, usually on foot, and often in running shoes. Her poems have been widely published in journals and very often involve a view from a towpath or a yearning for wide skies.

Kate Noakes' most recent collection is *The Filthy Quiet* (Parthian, 2019). She is an elected member of the Welsh Academy of Letters and her website www.boomslangpoetry.blogspot.com is archived by the National Library of Wales. She lives in London, where she acts as a trustee for literature advocacy organisation Spread the Word

Ben Norris is a poet, playwright and actor from Nottingham. A keen distance runner in his teens, with a particularly masochistic love of the mud, Ben represented GB at the 2010 World Cross Country Championships and had his sights set on a career in the sport before numerous injuries forced him to quit. 2018 saw him rediscover his love of running, and the spiritual role it played in his life alongside the physical one.

Verity Ockenden is a chef and elite athlete and runs to question the limits of her body and her mind. Her poetry is a tool with which to aid performance, by visualising her journey in the most memorable way possible. She likes to arrive breathless at hilltops, usually Win Green, with naught left in her lungs for the view to rob. To arrive home with bullion for legs, hungry for bread, ink and paper.

Jatinder Padda has been running her usual routes for almost twenty years, having read the blurb for Prozac Nation and figuring there was a better path to contentment. Her first memories of running are chasing siblings around the house and garden, then the sweet relief of missing team sports and doing cross-country runs during PE lessons. As an adult, she has pounded many asphalt, concrete, and muddy tracks, and ran her first marathon in 2018.

Scott Palmieri is a professor of English at Johnson & Wales University in Providence, Rhode Island. His writing has been published in *Sport Literate*, *Aethlon*, *Hobart*, *The Leaflet*, and *The Alembic*. Most of his running has been on baseball diamonds, and he will continue to play, as long as his legs allow. He resides in Wakefield, Rhode Island, with his wife and three children, his biggest fans.

Marie Papier has attended 5 years of the London Poetry School. Some of her poems are published in *The North*, *Agenda* and in Arvon/*Daily Telegraph*. She is a member of Stanza in Bristol. She actually prefers walking to running – a good way of taking in the landscape, seascape, and the riches of this beautiful country.

Sarah Passingham's father died May 2003 and although she didn't start running until October she felt there was a connection. Learning to run in your mid-forties isn't easy. She slowly improved, running cross-country and writing to smooth the grief; the two things became part of life. Her family memoir *Push: My Father, Polio, and Me* is published by Gatehouse Press, 2019.

Alan Payne was a sprinter, years ago. He was always third leg in the school relay team, running the bend, blue and white spikes making him feel he was floating on air even when, lungs bursting, he was watching a friend waiting for him to hit his mark before shooting off, arm stretched back, hand open, palm up. All so simple. No mixed feelings. No divided loyalties. No waking in the dark in the night. His pamphlet *Exploring the Orinoco* is published by Smith|Doorstop'

M R Peacocke grew up in South Devon. She had written poems since childhood, but it was only in her fifties that she began publishing seriously. Peterloo Poets published four collections: *Marginal Land* (1988), *Selves* (1995), *Speaking of the Dead* (2003) and *In Praise of Aunts* (2007), and *Caliban Dancing* was published by Shoestring Press in 2013. *Broken Ground: New and Selected Poems* was published by Shoestring in 2015, followed by *Finding the Planes* in 2018. *Honeycomb* was published by HappenStance Press in 2018. Several of her poems have won major prizes, and in 2005 she received a Cholmondeley Award.

Stuart Pickford has a Parkrun in his town. One Saturday morning, he asked the two people who always seemed to come last if they were disheartened. They replied that they hadn't come last, the people who had stayed in bed had come last. Stuart doesn't do many organised runs, he prefers to get out on his own – don't take a watch, don't count the miles, don't collate the data; get your head up and enjoy the sky, enjoy the day.

Pindar (c.518-438 BC) was an Ancient Greek lyric poet from Thebes.

Wendy Pratt is a poet, playwright and freelance writer living on the Yorkshire coast. She is an appalling runner with a terrible gait and no natural ability. She has run the Great North Run twice, in memory of her daughter who died in 2010. On both occasions she thought she wouldn't make it across the finish line. But she did. She hopes she never stops surprising herself, and that her toenails will eventually grow back.

Estelle Price had rarely run until a year ago. Now she has the kit and the motivational app and once, just once, ran 5k. Running and Estelle are in a relationship (although currently on a break) of shifting love and hate. On Lindow Common jogging round the rushes of Black Lake with the sun dipping and moorhens bobbing, they are lovers. Along the grass verge of Alderley Road at rush hour she only thinks of ending it.

Diana Moen Pritchard was born England in 1946, raised in Northern British Columbia, Canada and currently lives in Guernsey. Walking through wilderness to school, running, skiing from an early age, she won inter-school trophies. Her marathons, including London, Dublin, The Seven Sisters, Beachy Head plus orienteering and cross-country running has phased into Nordic walking. Keen poet, she published a pamphlet *Wool-gathering* in 2000, is featured in anthologies including *Reach*, *Second Light*, *Artemis* and *Ver Poets*, and regularly attends ICE Masterclasses in Cambridge.

Terry Quinn ran on beaches at Great Yarmouth, Abu Dhabi and Liverpool in his career as a Medical Engineer. He did the Highland Cross when working at Inverness Hospital. The River Ribble path took the place of sand until prolapsed discs did for him. His collection *The Amen of Knowledge* (2012) and a joint collection with Julie Maclean, *To Have To Follow* (2016) are published by Indigo Dreams Press. He runs the monthly Damson Poets in Preston.

Lynne Rees started running at 56. Family health issues were the initial motivation but she discovered an unexpected passion for it, on trails and road, from her first 5K to her last half-marathon. She's now the fittest she's been in her whole life, running the lanes and footpaths in rural Kent, and the coastline and mountains in Port Talbot, South Wales, with a joyful curiosity for the shapes made on Garmin maps.

Anne Ryland started running at the age of 54, after joining the inspirational Tweed Striders Walk-Jog programme, and recently completed her first 10k. Running solo along river and sea at dawn has deepened her affinity with the northern landscape. Her mother was disabled through adult life, so each run represents gratitude for and celebration of a healthy body. Her poetry collections are *Autumnologist*, shortlisted for The Forward Prize for Best First Collection, and *The Unmothering Class*.

Peter Sansom is a poet and tutor. His publications include *On the Pennine Way* (Littlewood, 1988) and *Everything You've Heard is True* (Carcanet, 1990), a Poetry Book Society Recommendation. His poem commissions include for *The Guardian*, *The Observer*, Radio Three, The Big Breakfast, a billboard in the centre of Lancaster and The Swedish Club (a Marine Insurers in Gothenburg). He taught the MA Poetry at Huddersfield for 10 years, was Fellow in Creative Writing at Leeds University. He is a director of The Poetry Business in Huddersfield, and co-editor of *The North* Magazine and Smith|Doorstop Books.

Elisabeth Sennitt Clough enjoys both poetry and running. She believes that both a run and a poem can be a struggle to complete sometimes, requiring different skill-sets, but with a similar sense of euphoria if the end-result is a good one. Favourite race: Boston USA Marathon. Favourite Poem: 'Prayer' by Carol Ann Duffy.

Di Slaney's poems have been anthologised and published in various magazines as well as being shortlisted for the Plough Prize and the Bridport Prize, and commended in the McLellan Prize. Two of her poems won joint first prize in the 2014 Brittle Star Poetry Competition and she won first prize in the 2015 Four Corners Poetry Competition. Her debut pamphlet collection *Dad's Slideshow* is available from Stonewood Press, and her first full collection *Reward for Winter* is available from Valley Press.

Morag Smith is an unathletic writer and European Scot. Her poetry has been published in anthologies and magazines, including *The Wild Word*, Speculative Books' *The View From Now* and *Crannog*. She started running in Germany while giving up smoking twenty years ago – the smoking stopped, the running followed her back to Scotland. It helps her think/stops her thinking and supports her recovery from the trauma of School Sports Day (don't ask).

Paul Stephenson grew up in Cambridge and studied modern languages. He took part in the Jerwood/Aldeburgh mentoring scheme in 2013/14. He has published three poetry pamphlets: *Those People* (Smith|Doorstop, 2015), which won the Poetry Business pamphlet competition judged by Billy Collins; *The Days that Followed Paris* (HappenStance, 2016), written after the Paris terrorist attacks of November 2015; and *Selfie with Waterlilies* (Paper Swans Press, 2017). He completed an MA in Creative Writing (Poetry) with the Manchester Writing School and is co-curating Poetry in Aldeburgh 2019.

Mandy Sutter used to enjoy taking part in 10K races. Nowadays she counts lampposts on a walk-one, run-one basis or walks on Ilkley Moor with her dog, sometimes breaking into a little jog. Her father, now 96, ran at White City Stadium when he was a boy.

Maria Taylor started running last year after years of vowing she wouldn't. She runs once or twice a week and is getting addicted. She hates running up the hill, but loves coming down. She is also a poet who has been published in various magazines, such as *Magma*, *The Rialto* and *The North*. Her most recent publication is *Instructions for Making Me*, published by Happen*Stance* Press

Barry Tench has had an uncomfortable history with running. From the curriculum torture of grammar school mud-splattered cross-country to the university freedom days of near complete fitness. Now in his 60th year he prefers solitary runs at dawn or dusk along the roads around his Shropshire home; an emotional return to the days of anxiety, when running felt like survival.

Ifor Thomas has been writing and running for as long as he can remember. He runs most days, whatever the weather or season, usually alone and close to the sea. Even when he runs the same route, the changing character of the sea and weather, renders the run unique. The rhythm of running releases creativity. Each run is a poem, perhaps haiku, sometimes epic. Even if it only ever exists in his head.

Pam Thompson is a writer and educator based in Leicester. Her second collection, *Strange Fashion*, was published by Pindrop Press in 2017. Pam is a 2019 Hawthornden Fellow. She runs to shake her mind free. She isn't bothered about personal bests but likes to think it helps to keep her fit. Sometimes she will run round the streets near her home, and round a Botanic Garden; at others, in Bradgate Park, Leicestershire, for all its different types of scenery.

Lizzy Turner had a seven-minute mile* as a gangly teenager. In the years between then and now, she ran only out of necessity. Now, she runs with her husband, who reveals the joy in things she never liked before. Kennington Park ("sprint finish!"), Bristol Harbour ("five more minutes!"), Westbury ("one last push to the end of this road!"). They ponder running as Mental Health Remedy – perhaps the remedy lies in company/support.
*"At altitude!!"

Iain Twiddy's poems have been published in *The Poetry Review*, *Poetry Ireland Review*, *The London Magazine*, *The Stinging Fly* and elsewhere. Having grown up in flat land, he enjoys running hills, but appreciates the spirit-lift that comes with running any terrain, whether forest, riverside or ice. His favourite place to run is Asahiyama, Sapporo, Japan.

Sarah Venart runs, lives and teaches in Montreal, Canada. Running eases the bridge between herself and the world at large; a good run every second day allows her to be an average mother and a more observant human being. Sarah's newest collection of poems, *I am the Big Heart*, comes out in 2020.

Rob Walton spent his childhood reading the print off his dad's Athletics Weekly magazines and waiting to run his first marathon. He gets ideas for poems and short stories running near the mouth of the Tyne and along the seafront near his home in Whitley Bay. A regular Parkrunner, he still dreams of entering the stadium to tumultuous cheers as he waves to the crowd during the last 385 yards.

Robert Walton's running days are over. He was always a team-games runner – football, rugby, etc – rather than a street-pounder, but a back problem brought his sport to an abrupt halt at 62. These days he spends marathon hours at the desk and is struggling to learn to play the saxophone. His second collection, *Sax Burglar Blues* (Seren), was recently shortlisted by *Wales Arts Review* for Welsh Books – the Best of 2018.

Matthew West is a writer based in Southampton who discovered running as an antidote to broken-heartedness while on holiday in the Lake District in 2015. Surprised into action on a swift descent of Yew Barrow, Matt developed a passion for fell-running and has since enjoyed ultra-pursuits in the mountains of England, Wales and North West Scotland.

Natalie Whittaker is a teacher and poet from South East London. She likes to run in the early evening, around Danson Park in Bexley, as the flocks of tropical parakeets come in to roost. Running gives her time to think after a busy day of teaching. Natalie got into running in her late twenties, which came as a bit of a shock as she hated PE at school. Now she can't imagine life without running.

Erin Wilson wondered if she had been knocked in the head when nearing mid-life. In order to figure this out, she picked herself up off the dining room table to walk through the woods. This, she found, wasn't fast enough. And so she began to move her feet faster. Running, like writing, is a way of being alive and assuring oneself of the verbdom of being. Lying on one's dining room table is death.

River Wolton is a reluctant runner who came last in the losers' race at primary school, and is proudly continuing that tradition, recently achieving 382nd out of 400 in her local 5k. The titles of her collections *Leap* and *Indoor Skydiving* (Smith|Doorstop) give the misleading impression that she is sporty, but her closest brush with competitive sport is a poem about pole-vaulting commissioned to celebrate the 2012 London Olympics.

Anna Woodford took up running in her 40s and recently lost her Great North Run virginity and nearly two toenails in the process. Her poetry collections are *Changing Room* (Salt, 2018) and *Birdhouse* (2010). She is a past winner of the Poetry Business competition and is Royal Literary Fellow at Newcastle University.

Acknowledgements

Thanks are due to the editors of the anthologies and magazines in which many of these poems have been published:

Abeer Ameer 'The Runner' in *The New Welsh Review*

Niall Campbell 'A New Father Thinks about Those Running Home' in *Prac-Crit*

Oliver Comins 'Jogging' in *iOTA*

Mike Farren 'Running with Simon' in *Un/Forced* (INGS Poetry, 2017)

Vicki Husband 'Something More Considerable' in *Beyond Boundaries* (Glasgow Libraries, 2018)

Rachael Mead 'The dog, the blackbird and the anxious mind' in *Meanjin* and *The Flaw in the Pattern* (UWAP, 2018)

Lynne Rees 'I am running through the wondrous silence of history' in *Blithe Spirit*, Journal of the British Haiku Society

Thanks also to the editors and publishers of the following books, where poems first appeared:

Jane Aspinall '10k' in *American Shadow* (Smith|Doorstop, 2010)

John Goodby 'The Tough of the Track' in *A True Prize* (Cinnamon Press, 2011)

Mark Granier 'Stopwatch' in *Fade Street* (Salt, 2007)

Tracey Herd 'What I Remember' in *Not in this World* (Bloodaxe, 2015)

Geoffrey Hill 'Watching the Boston Marathon' in *The Triumph of Love* (Penguin, 2007)

A E Housman 'To an Athlete Dying Young' in *A Shropshire Lad* (1896)

Igor Klikovac 'Gratitude to Big Cities' in *Stockholm Syndrome*, translated by John McAuliffe and Igor Klikovac (Smith|Doorstop, 2018)

Helen Mort 'Fox Miles' and 'Coffin Path' in *Division Street* (Chatto & Windus, 2013)

M R Peacock 'Running' in *Honeycomb* (HappenStance, 2018)

Pindar 'Olympian XI' in *Pindar's Victory Songs*, translated by Frank Nisetich (John Hopkins University Press, 1980)

Wendy Pratt 'Godsong' and 'Fuck You' in *Gifts the Mole Gave Me* (Valley Press, 2017)

Peter Sansom 'Cross Country' in *Careful What You Wish For* (Carcanet, 2015)

Di Slaney 'Bildr's Thorp' in *Reward for Winter* (Valley Press, 2016)

Pam Thompson 'Running, Anglesey, Easter' and 'The Run' in *Show Date and Time* (Smith|Doorstop, 2006)

Natalie Whittaker 'The ring-necked parakeets of South East London' in *Shadow Dogs* (ignitionpress, 2018)

Anna Woodford 'Bedsocks; Willow' in *Changing Room* (Salt, 2018)

Index of poems and first lines

4 miles   54

10k   58

20180611   54

After a 10k run and 9 years   111

After birth, I'd sit on a rubber ring – the sort   95

All my sadness went into my hips   102

All told, there wasn't much I understood   59

All winter we drove to Forches Cross: 68

Alnitak, Alnilam and Mintaka   55

A Local Legend   30

along the ramparts, under the gate and away   138

And I know that if I turn right, and then another   80

A New Father Thinks About Those Running Home   59

An Exercise in How to Move On   100

are screaming and green;   61

A run up to the course of love   32

As a child he was whipped for it,   130

As if there were fireflies awake at dawn   86

as much as the feeling I loved the facts   88

At the age when athletes retire, running called   134

Autumn Run   77

A woman who follows her own trail   115

Battle Cry   38

Beat, bum, rubber hoof, piston fist,   75

Bedsocks; Willow   111

Begin by leaving yourself behind; forget what you know   25

Big Heart   88

Bildr's thorp   128

Blake on his morning run sees angels in a tree   130

Blessing at the Allotments   71

can be recognised in various ways;   24

Cicadas unlashed their thunderous Morse   126

Climb as high   38

Coach   68

Coffin Path   65

Counting hawks like magpies; three for a girl   28

Cross Country   46

Cross Country   48

Culbin Forest 5K   135

DASH   98

Death turns, runs backwards, bouncing high   94

Dogs   123

Early Cretaceous, gentle jog amongst tree ferns and a herd of grazing Iguano-don.   26

Early Start, Winter Run. impression sequence   66

Eight Hundred Metres   35

escaped from their bodies | they run downhill   80

Evening Out   79

Every week, half past six we gather;   33

Fall and a sprinkling of snow.   72

Flight   122

Forest Run   72

Fox Miles   55

Fragility   103

from Olympian XI (Pindar's Victory Songs)   53

from Watching the Boston Marathon   115

Fuck You   30

George Rogan hadn't missed many dinners,   91

Ghosts   80

Give me five more years of running and I   92

God adds a small stone to the summit cairn,   70

Godsong   76

Gratitude to Big Cities   63

Grey stone, pebble-dashed;   78

Hainault Road   105

Having had the same legs. Having had the same body. Having had the   139

He doesn't live inside me I think as I run past cigarette can,   135

He ran from the farm like he was learning to slay, 128

he who undertakes to be a huntsman to a lord or gentleman 27

He won every race he entered; 90

Hill 58

His breathing deepens, starting a first circuit 57

Hitting the Berlin Wall 38

how 115

*I am running through the wondrous
silence of history* 42

I Believe You Still Have My Key 135

I bring us here to run away. 124

I can't run up the stairs, 32

I feel the swirl from Irma's skirts 77

I find running helps, 100

If it was just about style and technique 35

I keep running through canyons, past houses, 28

I know a man who runs every day, 30

I left Oromia as I was 116

I'm eleven though from my height 37

I'm learning a new language 119

I'm the one dressed for a ritual 71

Inevitable 137

In my treads 75

In Sickness and In Health 80

In the surgical brilliance of the opening lap 99

Into half light I run, up to the canal. 76

Introductions 11

In winter, my father sets up base camp 127

I perform the preparation rituals 93

I ran today with Amy Winehouse. What 137

I sat next to a TV strongman once. 38

is not the race itself but the evening 25

I still have the spike spanner that I used 109

It's 8 o'clock: I'm out enjoying 67

It's not every day 110

It's so cold my teeth ache 96

It starts with an elderly woman in a long black dress   89

it's when the body is at its most like a machine that the mind is at its least like a machine   105

I went out into the heat and ran down the sidewalk under the Sewing   54

Jogging   57

Just as autumn gave way to winter   58

Lane Discipline   45

Lap   23

Looking out from the steps of Black Sail Pass   79

Lose the trail of prayers that hang   76

Losing It   35

M25, turning   124

Maren   98

Mile Time   28

Mist below in the valley, you tempt me   58

Morning Run   67

My feet play the skin of the earth like a drum,   107

my old faithful friend   108

Night drops like a black stone   130

Night Run   23

Night Run, Mount Merrion, 1975   97

Notice how this bit of the Dighty slows,   70

Not running but failing   101

Not sure when she hit the wall;   104

of South East London   61

Old Trail Runner   127

On a pavement between fast cars   105

Once I ran and the bracing damp air   34

Once there was running, a spurt of joy   101

once you're on you can't get off   136

On hearing I've taken up running, my brother mentions fish oil,   56

On Running   34

On the edge of her shadow   35

On the tops   64

On Winning the Marathon at Sixty   86

Our faces cold water splashed and just out of bed, 135

Outdoor drum solo 107

Over fifty now, one of those joggers who pass, 46

Parkrun 40

Passing under the lime tree 132

past standing stones, invisible tombs, the path Chaucer's pilgrims took 42

People Who Go Running 24

phantom runner 73

Re-Run 89

Run 41

Run 60

Run, Boorana, Run ... 116

Run for your life 86

Runners in Town 33

Runners slip through the crowd, nip 33

Running 101

Running 119

Running – a bucket list 26

Running Advice 56

Running after dark in Homa Bay County 130

Running Against Wordsworth 74

Running, Anglesey, Easter 78

Running as Birdsong 139

Running Away 129

Running In The Family 126

Running, Like an Old Flame 134

running on a treadmill in the gym 102

Running on Silloth Beach on Christmas Day 28

Running Pacts 92

Running Together in Greenwich Park 124

Running with Mums 95

Running with Simon, 1983 95

run your body free of small hands 86

Sacramento 54

School Run 69

Set my watch running, check my gloves and hat 66

Sewage   132

She fell for a lover of miles,   45

Snails   127

So many hypotheses he cracked & cracked,   131

Someone else's bum   120

Something more considerable   25

Sometimes men need the winds most,   53

Soon the body quietens and the heart   74

so run   105

Spanner Skills   109

Spider   92

Spring Run   75

Sprint   37

Sprinter   90

Stopwatch   46

Sunday, on the run   138

Sunday. The road through Slippery Ford all yours   64

Sunny September Days   94

Supple as a dream I can't call back,   55

Suppose in the rain when you run   23

*Tempting the Runner Off the Green Circular,
Dundee*   70

Tenderised meat, hedonists, ambulances run through our veins. **Go for**   103

That impulse – to strip and sprint   97

That summer of drought, months   98

Thawing River   123

The Canal Path   76

The changing room smarts with old sweat and Deep Heat   46

The dog sleeps on the couch as if he's crash-landed.   67

The dog, the blackbird and the anxious mind   67

The Ex-Convict Runs a 10k   117

*The Experienced Huntsman. With instructions for Hunting the Buck, the Hare, the
Fox, the Badger, the Marten, and the Otter (1780)*   27

The Gap   91

The Middle Miles   99

The Result is What You See Today   62

There's virtue in the air, I sniff it,   41

The ring-necked parakeets   61

The rite of autumn   93

The Run   118

The Runner   104

These shoes used to wait for feet that climbed mountains   107

The Song of the Ungirt Runners   19

The thought of it has trailed me all day   23

The time you won your town the race   85

The Tough of the Track: an Alf Tupper triptych   42

The Tuesday night joggers   33

The Ultra Runner   70

The valley is open   62

They called me Spider when I ran   92

They said   129

This is where I run, it's near my house, the sky is flung wide here for a town –
for a time.   120

This might be a good place to pitch   53

This one, knobbled and red from the tow-path.   75

This thaw, a lit Saturday afternoon,   123

This was before I bought that record: 95

Thornes Park, Wakefield   47

Those days when all pages are empty   63

Those streets I ran with my dad   127

Thread Lines   133

Three yellow balls on a riverbank,   55

To an Athlete Dying Young   85

to my red tracksuit top   108

Trainers   107

trajectory   72

Treadmill   102

Tritina for My Hips   102

Twelve Reasons Why Not   123

Unhalting   131

Urban Wildlife   110

We need more words for mud: 47

We swing ungirded hips,   19
What I Remember   25
When I think of running   122
When I was but a child   101
When the moment feels right   133
When the runner in his high-vis vest   40
when walking down to the village today   73
Where else but here,   117
Who'd jog along the Coffin Path?   65
Winter Training   96
Woman Running Alone   115
Yes, I'm fat, with a crooked nose   30
Yes Tor Hill Race   53
You catch a dozing whippet unawares.   60
You didn't ask anything of me, just head-down ahead   48
you'd think tiring yourself out would   136
You gave me your camellia flower, bright as a shepherd's warning.   69
You kipped in the scullery of Aunt Meg's back-to-back   42
You run, or start to, taking on the night again.   118
You saw so much romance in competition,   98